I0646662

This is no longer
the property of
King County Library System

NOV 1 8 2009

REDMOND REGIONAL LIBRARY

OCT   2009

INTRODUCING
ISSUES WITH
OPPOSING
VIEWPOINTS®

Genetically Modified Food

Jennifer L. Skancke, *Book Editor*

GREENHAVEN PRESS
A part of Gale, Cengage Learning

GALE
CENGAGE Learning™

Detroit • New York • San Francisco • New Haven, Conn • Waterville, Maine • London

KING COUNTY LIBRARY SYSTEM, WA

Christine Nasso, *Publisher*
Elizabeth Des Chenes, *Managing Editor*

© 2009 Greenhaven Press, a part of Gale, Cengage Learning

Gale and Greenhaven Press are registered trademarks used herein under license.

For more information, contact:
Greenhaven Press
27500 Drake Rd.
Farmington Hills, MI 48331-3535
Or you can visit our Internet site at gale.cengage.com

ALL RIGHTS RESERVED.
No part of this work covered by the copyright herein may be reproduced, transmitted, stored, or used in any form or by any means graphic, electronic, or mechanical, including but not limited to photocopying, recording, scanning, digitizing, taping, Web distribution, information networks, or information storage and retrieval systems, except as permitted under Section 107 or 108 of the 1976 United States Copyright Act, without the prior written permission of the publisher.

For product information and technology assistance, contact us at

Gale Customer Support, 1-800-877-4253
For permission to use material from this text or product, submit all requests online at
www.cengage.com/permissions

Further permissions questions can be emailed to permissionrequest@cengage.com

Articles in Greenhaven Press anthologies are often edited for length to meet page requirements. In addition, original titles of these works are changed to clearly present the main thesis and to explicitly indicate the author's opinion. Every effort is made to ensure that Greenhaven Press accurately reflects the original intent of the authors. Every effort has been made to trace the owners of copyrighted material.

Cover Image Copyright Niderlader, 2008. Used under license from ShutterStock.com.

LIBRARY OF CONGRESS CATALOGING-IN-PUBLICATION DATA

Genetically modified food / Jennifer L. Skancke, book editor.
    p. cm. — (Introducing issues with opposing viewpoints)
  Includes bibliographical references and index.
  ISBN 978-0-7377-4273-2 (hardcover)
  1. Genetically modified foods. I. Skancke, Jennifer. II. Friedman, Lauri S. III. Series.
  TP248.65.F66G45745 2009
  664—dc22

                                                                        2008031909

Printed in the United States of America
1 2 3 4 5 6 7 12 11 10 09 08

Contents

Chapter 3: What Effects Do Genetically Modified Crops Have on the Environment?

Foreword

Indulging in a wide spectrum of ideas, beliefs, and perspectives is a critical cornerstone of democracy. After all, it is often debates over differences of opinion, such as whether to legalize abortion, how to treat prisoners, or when to enact the death penalty, that shape our society and drive it forward. Such diversity of thought is frequently regarded as the hallmark of a healthy and civilized culture. As the Reverend Clifford Schutjer of the First Congregational Church in Mansfield, Ohio, declared in a 2001 sermon, "Surrounding oneself with only like-minded people, restricting what we listen to or read only to what we find agreeable is irresponsible. Refusing to entertain doubts once we make up our minds is a subtle but deadly form of arrogance." With this advice in mind, Introducing Issues with Opposing Viewpoints books aim to open readers' minds to the critically divergent views that comprise our world's most important debates.

Introducing Issues with Opposing Viewpoints simplifies for students the enormous and often overwhelming mass of material now available via print and electronic media. Collected in every volume is an array of opinions that captures the essence of a particular controversy or topic. Introducing Issues with Opposing Viewpoints books embody the spirit of nineteenth-century journalist Charles A. Dana's axiom: "Fight for your opinions, but do not believe that they contain the whole truth, or the only truth." Absorbing such contrasting opinions teaches students to analyze the strength of an argument and compare it to its opposition. From this process readers can inform and strengthen their own opinions, or be exposed to new information that will change their minds. Introducing Issues with Opposing Viewpoints is a mosaic of different voices. The authors are statesmen, pundits, academics, journalists, corporations, and ordinary people who have felt compelled to share their experiences and ideas in a public forum. Their words have been collected from newspapers, journals, books, speeches, interviews, and the Internet, the fastest growing body of opinionated material in the world.

Introducing Issues with Opposing Viewpoints shares many of the well-known features of its critically acclaimed parent series, Opposing Viewpoints. The articles are presented in a pro/con format, allowing readers to absorb divergent perspectives side by side. Active reading questions preface each viewpoint, requiring the student to approach the material thoughtfully and carefully. Useful charts, graphs, and cartoons supplement each article. A thorough introduction provides readers with crucial background on an issue. An annotated bibliography points the reader toward articles, books, and Web sites that contain additional information on the topic. An appendix of organizations to contact contains a wide variety of charities, nonprofit organizations, political groups, and private enterprises that each hold a position on the issue at hand. Finally, a comprehensive index allows readers to locate content quickly and efficiently.

Introducing Issues with Opposing Viewpoints is also significantly different from Opposing Viewpoints. As the series title implies, its presentation will help introduce students to the concept of opposing viewpoints and learn to use this material to aid in critical writing and debate. The series' four-color, accessible format makes the books attractive and inviting to readers of all levels. In addition, each viewpoint has been carefully edited to maximize a reader's understanding of the content. Short but thorough viewpoints capture the essence of an argument. A substantial, thought-provoking essay question placed at the end of each viewpoint asks the student to further investigate the issues raised in the viewpoint, compare and contrast two authors' arguments, or consider how one might go about forming an opinion on the topic at hand. Each viewpoint contains sidebars that include at-a-glance information and handy statistics. A Facts About section located in the back of the book further supplies students with relevant facts and figures.

Following in the tradition of the Opposing Viewpoints series, Greenhaven Press continues to provide readers with invaluable exposure to the controversial issues that shape our world. As John Stuart Mill once wrote: "The only way in which a human being can make some approach to knowing the whole of a subject is by hearing what can be said about it by persons of every variety of opinion and studying all modes in which it can be looked at by every character of mind. No wise man ever acquired his wisdom in any mode but this." It is to this principle that Introducing Issues with Opposing Viewpoints books are dedicated.

Introduction

Genetically modified (GM) foods are just one of many technological advances shaping the way the world thinks about food and agriculture in the twenty-first century. As the world's population exponentially increases, fears of food shortages, coupled with the destruction of important croplands, have spawned government officials, scientists, and entrepreneurs who look for new, groundbreaking ways to meet world food demands—this search has resulted in the creation of genetically modified food.

Genetically modified food comes from organisms that have had their DNA altered through genetic engineering. In most cases, one organism's DNA is inserted into another's to produce useful genetic traits, such as being pest-resistant, more flavorful, or requiring less water. Although scientists have been experimenting with genetic modification since the early 1900s, it was not until the 1990s that biotech companies began growing genetically engineered crops commercially. The first GM food product to hit stores was a tomato called the "Flavr Savr." The Flavr Savr was engineered to be hardier and less prone to rotting. Next, biotech companies began modifying soybeans, corn, cotton, maize, and grape seed varieties. Most of these crops were engineered to be insect resistant or herbicide tolerant—that is, they were genetically built to contain genes that deflected attacks from pests and/or genes that allowed crops to be sprayed with poison that would kill pests and weeds but not the crop itself. Because of their reduced vulnerability to pesticides and insects, genetically modified crops yield more food than regular crops and have become more popular to plant: Between 1995 and 2005, the total area of land used to grow GM crops increased from 4.2 million acres to 222 million acres worldwide.

While some countries have embraced genetically modified foods, others have vehemently resisted them. In Europe, for example, consumers became wary of genetically modified foods after several reports indicated they were not fit for human consumption. In one study by the Rowett Research Institute in Scotland, a GM potato modified with an insecticide gene was found to be toxic to rats. In another study published in the British medical journal *Lancet*, scientists reported that rats fed GM food experienced depressed immune systems, inflammation of the intestines, and altered vital organs. Finally, the discovery that allergy-triggering proteins can be passed from one organism to another during genetic modification has further heightened people's skepticism of GM food.

These were just some of many reasons the majority of European consumers have denounced genetically modified organisms. According to a 2005 Eurobarometer poll, 54 percent of European consumers believe GM food is dangerous for human consumption. Even the European Commission (EU) declared that the attitude toward GM products should be one of extreme caution. In fact, in 1998 the EU suspended the use of genetically modified organisms (GMOs) in the food supply. The EU lifted the ban in 2004 after it introduced some new rules, such as requiring all products that contain GM foods to be labeled (both so that consumers can be aware of what they eat, and also so all products containing genetically modified organisms can be traced in the event a recall is necessary). Despite the new regulations Europeans remain skeptical, says a Friends of the Earth campaigner: "There is no future for genetically modified food or crops in Europe. Politicians may be saying yes but the public is clearly saying no. The European market is virtually dead, regions are banning the growing of GM crops and the industry is packing up and leaving."

But perhaps no rejection of GM food has been as shocking as that of drought-stricken Zambia, an African nation that in 2002 rejected tons of food aid from the United States because the food contained genetically modified ingredients. Despite having nearly 3 million starving citizens, Zambia rejected the desperately needed aid because it deemed the threat to its people from GM food was greater than that of starvation. Indeed, officials and citizens were concerned that the GM food aid not only threatened their health and safety but, because of the way GM crops and seeds tend to dominate and even obliterate non-GM crops and seeds, their livelihoods as farmers. As the charity Action Aid, which opposes the introduction of GM seeds into Africa, warned: "Rather than reducing world hunger, genetic engineering is likely to exacerbate it. Farmers will be caught in a vicious circle, increasingly dependent on a small number of giant multinationals" to sell them seeds, rather than being able to be dependent on their own seeds to grow food.

While the response to GM foods has been mostly negative in Europe and places in Africa, other nations, such as the United States, Argentina, Canada, Brazil, and China have been much more accepting of it. Indeed, with more than 142 million acres of GM crops planted in the United States, millions of Americans eat GM food every day. In fact, the Grocery Manufacturers of America estimates that 75 percent of products on grocery store shelves contain some form of GMO. Because it believes GM food to be safe, the U.S. government does not require GM products to be labeled, and only a minority of American consumers have expressed concern over the lack of labeling.

Furthermore, supporters of the technology claim that because GM hysteria is not scientifically justified, poor, starving people are needlessly rejecting it at their own peril. When African nations began rejecting GM food in 2002, officials from a wide variety of agencies and institutions warned them not to, claiming they were worsening the problem of hunger in their countries. Indeed, crops that grow faster, persevere under more difficult growing conditions, and are more nutritious are seen by some to only help ease conditions of hunger, as one BBC News reporter observed: "Many African scientists believe genetically modified (GM) crops offer the only hope of avoiding mass starvation on the continent." Furthermore, some genetic engineering techniques can insert vitamins and minerals into food crops, a further nutritional boost for starving people. Because of all these factors, the International Food Policy Research Institute (IFPRI) and other hunger and development organizations claim that nations that reject GM food are losing out and only hurting themselves.

What role genetically modified foods will play in battling world hunger has yet to be determined. But as the world's population increases and valuable farmland and resources are depleted, it will be necessary for all nations of the world to work together on the global food crisis. Examining the way the world has responded to genetically modified food is just one of the many issues explored in *Introducing Issues with Opposing Viewpoints: Genetically Modified Food.* Readers will also consider arguments about whether genetically modified food is safe for human consumption, whether it can alleviate world hunger, and what potential benefits and consequences GM crops pose to the environment. Readers will examine these questions in the article pairs and conclude for themselves if genetically modified foods should be embraced or rejected by the world.

Chapter 1

Is Genetically Modified Food Safe?

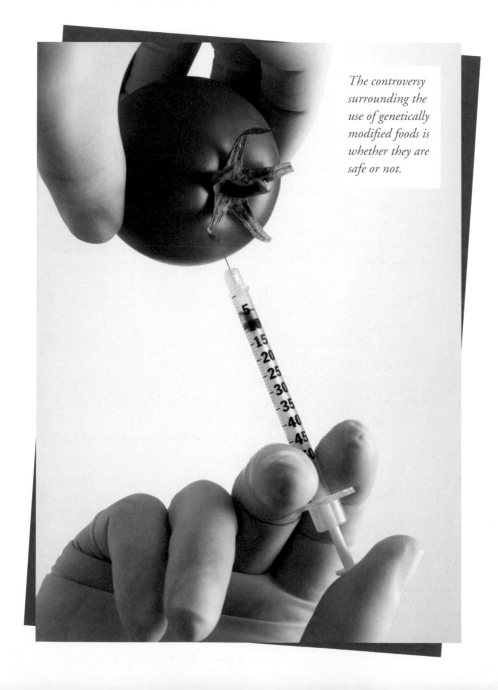

The controversy surrounding the use of genetically modified foods is whether they are safe or not.

Genetically Modified Food Is Safe

Mark I. Schwartz

"There is now abundant scientific evidence, from countless independent studies, that biotech crops and foods are safe . . . and improve basic nutrition."

In the following viewpoint Mark I. Schwartz argues that genetically modified food crops are safe for human consumption. According to the author, large percentages of America's soybeans, cotton, and corn come from seeds that have been genetically modified. In fact, Schwartz says that over 75 percent of the processed food sold in supermarkets contains some form of genetically modified food. Few safety or health problems have resulted from the consumption of these foods, claims Schwartz. To prove his case, he cites studies undertaken by the Food and Drug Administration (FDA) that found genetically modified food to be very safe. Schwartz concludes that consumers should feel confident that genetically modified food is safe and healthy.

Schwartz practices food and drug law in the Washington, DC area.

Mark I. Schwartz, "Genetically Safer; Europe Continues to Resist Genetically Modified Crops, Though They're Actually Safer than Conventional Ones," *National Post*, February 13, 2008, p. FP15. Copyright © National Post Company. Reproduced by permission.

AS YOU READ, CONSIDER THE FOLLOWING QUESTIONS:
1. What percentage of America's soybeans, cotton, and corn crops are genetically engineered, according to the author?
2. According to the author, the U.S. Food and Drug Administration found what to be true of all seventy of the genetically engineered products it tested?
3. Genetically modified corn contains how many fewer fungal toxins than non–genetically engineered corn, according to the author?

L ast week [the first week in February 2008], France filed a request with the European Union [EU] to formally ban the commercial use of "MON 810", a variety of corn developed by Monsanto, the U.S. biotech firm. This corn variety was the only genetically modified [GM] crop grown in the French nation, and one of only two approved for cultivation in the EU. The Union and its member states have long raised concerns about the safety of biotech foods, despite substantial scientific evidence contradicting these concerns, and have effectively precluded the cultivation or sale of biotech crops or foods anywhere on the continent.

Several years ago, Canada, the United States and Argentina formally lodged a complaint with the World Trade Organization [WTO], arguing that there was no scientific evidence to justify the EU's effective ban on biotech foods, and that it was an unfair barrier to companies that wanted to export to Europe. In 2006, the WTO agreed, and deemed the restrictions imposed on biotech foods by European countries to be illegal. The EU has yet to comply with the global trade body's ruling.

On the other hand, in North America, dozens of new crops and foods resulting from recombinant DNA technology have been marketed over the past decade, and they have been an overwhelming success. Indeed, fully 90% of the soybeans currently planted in the U.S. are of a biotech variety, and close to 80% of cotton and 60% of corn are of a biotech variety. Furthermore, fully three-quarters of the processed foods in our supermarkets contain ingredients from recombinant DNA modified plants.

Genetically Modified Foods Have Many Benefits

The seamless integration of biotech foods into our food supply has its origin in the Co-ordinated Framework for Regulation of Biotechnology, a document that laid the groundwork for establishing that the characteristics of the end-product determine the risk level, and hence the level of regulation, rather than the characteristics of the process by which the end-product is developed. This conclusion is based on the fact that the genes of virtually all organisms consist of DNA and, scientifically speaking, it's what the DNA produces, not where it comes from, that matters. The result is that biotech foods here are effectively regulated no differently than conventional foods. Furthermore, because the end product, not the process, determines the level of risk, biotech foods are generally not labelled any differently than conventional foods.

The relative importance of regulating the process (as in the EU) instead of the end product is referred to as the "process-product paradigm." With 10 years of hindsight to guide us, which is the better regulatory framework? Whether we compare these products

In 2007 the FDA tested and evaluated seventy biotech food products and found all to be as safe as their natural counterparts.

on the basis of their production costs, diversity of new varietals, or safety, the clear winner is end-product regulation of biotech crops and foods.

For instance, farmers who have used crops containing genes enhancing resistance to pests have significantly reduced their reliance on pesticides, and simultaneously increased their yields. For cotton plants alone, the net financial gain to American farmers has been in the hundreds of millions of dollars. Also, one of the most promising areas of new crop development involves the marketing of genetically engineered plant varieties carrying traits to improve basic nutrition, particularly in the Third World, by increasing the crops' content of essential minerals and vitamins.

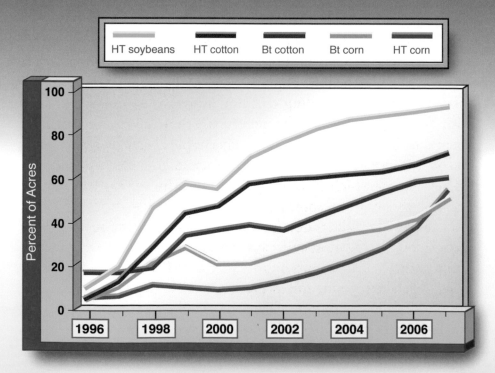

Genetically Modified Crops in the United States

Each year, genetically modified crops are increasingly planted in the United States. Popular herbicide-resistant (HT) and insect-resistant (Bt) crops include soybeans, corn, and cotton.

HT soybeans   HT cotton   Bt cotton   Bt corn   HT corn

Percent of Acres

100
80
60
40
20
0

1996   1998   2000   2002   2004   2006

Taken from: USDA, Economic Research Service, and Jorge Fernandez-Cornejo, *Amber Waves;* Sep 2007; 5, 4; ABI/INFORM Global.

Conventional Crops Can Be Less Safe than GM Crops

As for safety, by the end of 2007, the U.S. Food and Drug Administration had evaluated approximately 70 biotech food products and found them all to be as safe as their conventional counterparts. Furthermore, a large body of independent scientific evidence confirms that there is nothing about biotech foods that causes them to be inherently more dangerous than foods made from conventional crops. For instance, a large study by the National Academy of Sciences evaluated the likelihood of unintended health effects as a result of various methods of developing new strains, and

FAST FACT

A 2008 report produced by the USDA, EPA, and FDA have concluded that no public health, food, or feed safety concerns exist with genetically modified crops.

concluded that mutagen breeding, a century-old "conventional" means of altering crops, was more likely to be genetically disruptive than any form of genetic engineering. Mutagen breeding also produced the widest range of unintended effects.

What many opponents of bioengineering refuse to acknowledge is that many traditional plant breeding techniques are simply imprecise forms of the very genetic engineering that they claim to reject. For instance, mutagen-breeding techniques involve bombarding plants with X-rays, gamma rays, fast neutrons, or one of a variety of toxic chemicals, in an attempt to induce favourable chromosomal changes and genetic mutations. These techniques are so imprecise that researchers never know which chromosomes they are disrupting, let alone the genes on these chromosomes that they are mutating.

Examples of products developed using these conventional methods include some of the most common varieties of grapefruit, watermelon, wheat, barley, rice, peanuts and lettuce, as well as hundreds of other fruits, vegetables, grains and legumes that are in supermarkets around the world. Indeed, not one of the foods produced through the use of mutagen breeding is labelled "mutagen bred" or "engineered using ionizing radiation or toxic chemicals."

GM Crops Can Have Fewer Toxins than Traditional Crops

Ironically, an increasing number of studies have concluded that biotech foods are actually healthier and safer in many respects than their conventional counterparts. Examples include some of the very products that France and the EU have banned, namely, varieties of biotech corn. Minute quantities of the fungal toxin Fumonisin have been linked to cancer, liver toxicity and neural tube defects in newborns. The principal way these toxins enter the food supply is via insect-damaged plants. Certain biotech crops, such as MON 810 (sold under the tradename of YieldGard), are engineered to produce a protein that is toxic to many boring insects, but perfectly safe to mammals, thereby substantially reducing damage to crops, which are the vehicle by which fungal toxins enter our food supply. These crops have been shown to contain 900% fewer fungal toxins than the non-GM corn varieties grown by organic and traditional farmers.

Indeed, these scientific conclusions have led to suggestions that health claims be allowed on these biotech varieties or that warning labels be mandated on certain conventional products, turning on its head the argument that bioengineered foods be labelled as "genetically engineered" in order to enable consumers to seek out the "safer" conventional products.

There is now abundant scientific evidence, from countless independent studies, that biotech crops and foods are safe, can lower production costs, reduce reliance on pesticides, and improve basic nutrition. If France and the other EU countries do not comply with the WTO's ruling deeming Europe's trade restrictions to be illegal, Canada and the United States will just leave the Europeans to toil on their own in what will eventually come to be known there as the dark ages of European science.

EVALUATING THE AUTHOR'S ARGUMENTS:

In this viewpoint not only does Mark I. Schwartz argue that genetically modified food is safe, but he suggests that it is actually conventional crops that pose a health risk. What does he mean by this, and what evidence does he offer to support his argument?

Genetically Modified Food Is Not Safe

Jeffrey M. Smith

"*Several studies and reports from the field provide evidence that GM foods are toxic.*"

In the following viewpoint Jeffrey M. Smith argues that genetically modified (GM) foods are unsafe for human consumption. Many genetically engineered plants contain a toxin known as "Bt," which is a pesticide that protects crops from predatory insects. Bt is engineered directly into genetically modified seeds; consequently, when humans consume GM foods, they ingest this toxin. Smith explains that human exposure to Bt when it is simply sprayed on non–genetically modified crops causes skin irritation, nausea, fever, altered consciousness, and even seizures. Furthermore, exposure to the Bt toxin can also lead to increased incidence of allergies and failed immune system response. Smith reasons that if these side effects occur from external spraying, health consequences are bound to result from consuming food that has Bt written into its genetic code.

Jeffrey M. Smith is a leading spokesperson on the health dangers of genetically modified organisms. He has written two books, *Seeds of Deception: Exposing Industry*

Jeffrey M. Smith, "Genetically Engineered Foods May Cause Rising Food Allergies," *Total Health*, vol. 29, November 2007, pp. 41–42. Reproduced by permission.

and Government Lies About the Safety of Genetically Engineered Foods and *Genetic Roulette: The Documented Health Risk of Genetically Engineered Foods.*

AS YOU READ, CONSIDER THE FOLLOWING QUESTIONS:
1. What does the author mean when he says that the genetically engineered "plant does the work, not the farmer?"
2. According to Smith, genetically modified crops produce how many more toxins than the pesticides used on traditionally grown crops?
3. What effect did the pollen of genetically engineered corn have on a village of Filipinos in 2003, according to the author?

The biotech industry is fond of saying they offer genetically modified (GM) crops that resist pests. This might conjure up the image of insects staying away from GM crop fields. But "resisting pests" is just a euphemism for contains its own built-in pesticide. When bugs take a bite of the GM plant, the toxins split open their stomach and kill them.

The idea that we consume that same toxic pesticide in every bite is hardly appetizing. But the biotech companies and the Environmental Protection Agency—which regulates plant produced pesticides—tell us not to worry. They contend that the pesticide called Bt *(Bacillus thuringiensis)* is produced naturally from a soil bacterium and has a history of safe use. Organic farmers, for example, have used solutions containing the natural bacteria for years as a method of insect control. Genetic engineers simply remove the gene that produces the Bt in bacteria and then insert it into the DNA of corn and cotton plants, so that the plant does the work, not the farmer. Moreover, they say that Bt-toxin is quickly destroyed in our stomach; and even if it survived, since humans and other mammals have no receptors for the toxin, it would not interact with us in any case.

These arguments, however, are just that—unsupported assumptions. Research tells a different story.

Bt Spray Is Dangerous to Humans
When natural Bt was sprayed over areas around Vancouver [Canada] and Washington State to fight gypsy moths, about 500 people report-

ed reactions—mostly allergy or flu-like symptoms. Six people had to go to the emergency room for allergies or asthma. Workers who applied Bt sprays reported eye, nose, throat, and respiratory irritation, and some showed an antibody immune response linked to Bt. Farmers exposed to liquid Bt formulations had reactions including infection, an ulcer on the cornea, skin irritation, burning, swelling, and redness. One woman who was accidentally sprayed with Bt also developed fever, altered consciousness, and seizures.

In fact, authorities have long acknowledged that "people with compromised immune systems or preexisting allergies may be particularly susceptible to the effects of Bt." The Oregon Health Division advises that "individuals with . . . physician-diagnosed causes of severe immune disorders may consider leaving the area during the actual spraying." A spray manufacturer warns, "repeated exposure via inhalation can result in sensitization and allergic response in hypersensitive individuals." So much for the contention that Bt does not interact with humans.

As for being thoroughly destroyed in the digestive system, mouse studies disproved this as well. Mice fed Bt-toxin showed significant immune responses—as potent as cholera toxin. In addition, the Bt caused their immune system to become sensitive to formerly harmless compounds. This suggests that exposure might make a person allergic

Genetically Modified Food May Cause Allergies

Genetically modified organisms such as corn and pesticide have caused mild to severe allergic reactions in some people.

	Upper Respiratory	Eyes	Skin	Overall
Bt Spray (genetically modified pesticide)	Sneezing, runny nose, exacerbations of asthma	Watery, red	Itching, burning, inflammation, red, swelling	Fever, some in hospital
Bt Cotton	Sneezing, runny nose	Watery, red	Itching, burning, eruptions, red, swelling	Fever, some in hospital

Taken from: Jeffrey M. Smith, "Genetically Modified Foods May Cause Rising Food Allergies," *Total Health*, vol. 29, no. 4, August–September 2007, p. 42.

to a wide range of substances. *The EPA's own expert advisors said that the mouse and farm worker studies above "suggest that Bt proteins could act as antigenic and allergenic sources."*

The Toxin in GM Plants Is More Dangerous than Natural Sprays

The Bt-toxin produced in GM crops is "vastly different from the bacterial [Bt-toxins] used in organic and traditional farming and forestry." First of all, GM plants produce about 3,000–5,000 times the amount of toxin as the sprays. And the spray form is broken down within a few days to two weeks by sunlight, high temperatures, or substances on the leaves of plants; and it can be "washed from leaves into the soil by rainfall," or rinsed by consumers. A Bt producing GM plant, on the other hand, continuously produces the toxin in every cell where it does not dissipate by weather and cannot be washed off.

FAST FACT

According to Japan's Nagoya University, genetically engineered "Roundup Ready" soybeans contain high concentrations of three toxic substances.

The natural toxin produced in bacteria is inactive until it gets inside the alkaline digestive tract of an insect. Once inside, a "safety catch" is removed and the Bt becomes toxic. But scientists change the sequence of the Bt gene before inserting it into GM plants. The Bt toxin it produces usually comes without the safety catch. The plant-produced Bt toxin is always active and more likely to trigger an immune response than the natural variety.

Bt-Toxin Fails Safety Studies

Tests cannot verify that a GM protein introduced into the food supply for the first time will not cause allergies in some people. The World Health Organization (WHO) and UN Food and Agriculture Organization (FAO) offer criteria designed to reduce the likelihood that allergenic GM crops are approved. They suggest examining a protein for 1) similarity of its amino acid sequence to known aller-

Studies have shown that repeated exposure to Bt can result in an allergic response in hypersensitive individuals.

gens, 2) digestive stability and 3) heat stability. These properties aren't predictive of allergenicity, but their presence, according to experts, should be sufficient to reject the GM crop or at least require more testing. The Bt-toxin produced in GM corn fails all three criteria.

For example, the specific Bt-toxin found in Monsanto's Yield Guard and Syngenta's Bt 11 corn varieties is called Cry1Ab. In 1998, an FDA researcher discovered that Cry1Ab shared a sequence of 9–12 amino acids with vitellogenin, an egg yolk allergen. The study concluded that "the similarity . . . might be sufficient to warrant additional evaluation." No additional evaluation took place.

Cry1Ab is also very resistant to digestion and heat. It is nearly as stable as the type of Bt-toxin produced by StarLink corn. StarLink was a GM variety not approved for human consumption because experts believed that its highly stable protein might trigger allergies. Although it was grown for use in animal feed, it contaminated the U.S. food supply in 2000. Thousands of consumers complained to food manufacturers about possible reactions and over 300 items were subject to recall. After the StarLink incident, expert advisors to the

EPA had called for "surveillance and clinical assessment of 'exposed individuals' to confirm the allergenicity of Bt products." Again, no such monitoring has taken place.

Bt Cotton Triggers Allergic Reactions

A 2005 report by medical investigators in India describes an ominous finding. Hundreds of agricultural workers are developing moderate or severe allergic reactions when exposed to Bt cotton. This includes those picking cotton, loading it, cleaning it, or even leaning against it. Some at a ginning factory must take antihistamines daily, in order to go to work. Reactions are only triggered with the Bt varieties. Furthermore, the symptoms are virtually identical to those described by the 500 people in Vancouver and Washington who were sprayed with Bt. Only "exacerbations of asthma" were in one list and not the other. (We are unaware of similar reports in the U.S., where 83 percent of the cotton is Bt. But in the U.S., cotton is harvested by machine, not by hand.)

The experience of the Indian workers begs the question, "How long does the Bt-toxin stay active in the cotton?" Is there any risk using cotton diapers, tampons, or bandages? In the latter case, if the Bt-toxin interfered with healing it could be a disaster. With diabetics, for example, unhealed wounds may be cause for amputation.

Cottonseed is also used for cottonseed oil—used in many processed foods in the U.S. The normal methods used to extract oil likely destroy the toxin, although cold pressed oil may still retain some of it. Other parts of the cotton plant, however, are routinely used as animal feed. . . .

Bt Corn Pollen May Cause Allergies

Bt-toxin is produced in GM corn and can be eaten intact. It is also in pollen, which can be breathed in. In 2003, during the time when an adjacent Bt cornfield was pollinating, virtually an entire Filipino village of about 100 people were stricken by a disease. The symptoms included headaches, dizziness, extreme stomach pain, vomiting, chest pains, fever and allergies, as well as respiratory, intestinal, and skin reactions. The symptoms appeared first in those living closest to the field, and then progressed to others by proximity. Blood samples from 39 individuals showed antibodies in response to Bt-toxin; this supports, but does not prove a link to the symptoms. When the same corn was planted in four other villages the following year, however, the symptoms returned in all four areas—only during the time of pollination. . . .

Allergic reactions are a defensive, often harmful immune system response to an external irritant. The body interprets something as foreign, different and offensive, and reacts accordingly. All GM foods, by definition, have something foreign and different. According to GM food safety expert Arpad Pusztai, "a consistent feature of all the studies done, published or unpublished . . . indicates major problems with changes in the immune status of animals fed on various GM crops/foods."

In addition to immune responses, several studies and reports from the field provide evidence that GM foods are toxic.

EVALUATING THE AUTHORS' ARGUMENTS:

The author of the previous viewpoint, Mark I. Schwartz, and the author of this one, Jeffrey M. Smith, come to very different conclusions about the safety of GM food. Write one paragraph that states each author's argument and the main pieces of evidence offered to support it. Then, state with which author you agree.

Viewpoint

3

Genetically Modified Food Can Cause Disease

Giuseppe Nacci

"[Genetically modified food] may make it completely impossible to cure tumors and other diseases."

In the following viewpoint Giuseppe Nacci argues that eating genetically modified food may cause disease in humans. Nacci explains that the human body is a complex system that depends on particular vitamins, proteins, and chemicals to function and remain healthy. Many diseases, especially cancer, result from a lack of vitamins or the poisoning of the body's systems by toxins. Given this, Nacci claims that eating genetically modified food elevates the risk of disease because it introduces people to foreign, toxic substances that alter their sensitive biochemical systems. These substances can inhibit the body's ability to fight disease, or in some cases, cause DNA mutations that trigger new diseases. In order to protect humans from an increased risk of disease, Nacci concludes that genetically modified food should not be a part of the human diet.

Nacci is an Italian physician.

Giuseppe Nacci, "The Threat of Genetically Modified Organisms (part I)," *Gerson Healing Newsletter,* vol. 21, May–June 2006, pp. 5–8. Copyright © 2006 The Gerson Institute. Reproduced by permission.

AS YOU READ, CONSIDER THE FOLLOWING QUESTIONS:
  1. According to Nacci, where do a majority of the genes used in genetically engineered foods come from?
  2. What effect might genetically modified vitamin molecules have on vegetable crops, according to the author?
  3. What effect does Nacci say genetically modified foods have on the treatment of cancer?

Cancer is a degenerative disease caused by a lack of vitamins and poisoning from chemical substances present in food. One can estimate the number of vitamins and pro-vitamin substances present in natural plants commonly used as food by humans, as more than 15,000 to 30,000. The introduction into modern agriculture of Genetically Modified Organisms (GMOs) is an unjustified and dangerous alteration of what evolution has produced in plants over hundreds of millions of years: plants on which the subsequent biochemical evolution of superior complex animal organisms has been based, culminating with the advent of mammals in the last 65 million years and then with the arrival of man. The delicate biochemical balance of the human race depends on plant species remaining integral, just as evolution created them, because the health of every one of us is based on the biochemical human cell, and this depends, through the complexity of the DNA, on the use of thousands of vitamins and of the herbal-chemical compounds present in nature.

Genetically Modified Foods Alter Human Biochemistry

To get maximum agricultural production today we resort to changing the genetic patrimony of natural plants, with the aim of changing their structure and making them sterile (thus farmers have to buy new seeds every year), patenting the transformation induced and re-selling the product all over the world. It has been stated that there is a substantial equivalence between the genetically modified product (GMO) and that obtained by selecting genetic characteristics (that is by means of naturally crossbreeding plants as has been done by man over the course of thousands of years). However the idea of

Seeds from GMO plants are said to lack the anticancer vitamin B17.

"substantial equivalence" cannot be supported, because the natural crossbreeding of plants uses seeds of the same species, while genetic manipulation (GMO) crosses all barriers, and introduces genes from other types of vegetable species or even bacteria, viruses and animal genes. In fact the majority of genes used in genetic engineering come from living species which have never been a part of the human food chain and actually come from the DNA not of plants but of animals, bacteria or viruses and/or transgenic retroviruses. As a doctor qualified in nuclear medicine the author has had the opportunity to study the effects of ionizing radiation on complex organisms for years. It is his personal view that plants, too, are complex organisms; every genetic modification caused by man (through radiation such as that emitted at Chernobyl [the Soviet nuclear power plant that experienced a disastrous meltdown in 1986], or viruses such as presently used in GMO), however small that modification may be, will cause damage, irreparable damage which often cannot be seen, because man has only discovered a limited number of safe vitamins and provitamin substances. There are, however, tens of thousands of vitamins and other substances present in plants, and it is these which are responsible for the correct functioning of the biochemical human complex and the human genome (DNA). . . .

Genetically Modified Food Disrupts the Body's Ability to Fight Disease

Vitamin and pro-vitamin compounds no longer present in foods, with the consequent increase in degenerative and deficiency diseases like cancer. On this subject, recent scientific research has shown that transgenic food causes the immune defense system of rats to collapse, with the subsequent appearance of tumors.

The deliberate attempt to deactivate the natural substances in plants (with Fortilin, Bcl-2, Bcl-xl) is, for example, very serious. These are vitamins which enter into the complex enzymatic mechanism of DNA in mammals, inducing the apoptosis (suicide) phenomenon in these mammals' cells if they are diseased through infection or other illnesses (such as cancer). This action of blocking apoptosis, introduced experimentally into the tobacco plant by means of a virus, is a serious act of deliberate damage inflicted on the ecosystem by means of GMO; damage which, if it is propagated on plants in commonly used foods, may make it completely impossible to cure tumors and other diseases by the methods considered in this study.

FAST FACT

According to Arpad Pusztai, a leading expert on GM foods, rats fed an experimental GM food developed immune system damage and other serious health problems in ten days.

In addition to the possible disappearance of anti-cancer vitamins that induce apoptosis (suicide) of tumors there is the elimination of seeds from GMO fruits. The importance of seeds as anti-cancer factors resides principally in the fact that they contain vitamins.

The big GMO seed companies are putting onto the world agricultural market fruits such as Cucumis melo, Citrus limonum, Citrullus vulgaris, Solanum lycopersicum, Vitis vinifera, without seeds to inflict deliberate damage on the ecosystem.

Genetically Modified Food May Create New Diseases

Because of the introduction of foreign genes (for example from animals, bacteria, viruses and retroviruses) into the DNA of plants, an alteration in the normal genomic sequence of the plant occurs, with the appearance of new proteins and/or the loss of other proteins from a genomic sequence. New substances similar to natural vitamins have appeared, but which actually have enzymatic and biochemical characteristics different from natural ones, and therefore impose changes in their biochemical activity on the human genome, once they have been introduced through food.

Hence there is the potential risk of new diseases of an "artificial" type, caused by the manipulation (GMO) of vegetable organisms, genetically polluted by new vitamin molecules with totally unknown inductive effects on the human DNA, but, given its extreme complexity and vulnerability, probably heralding serious damage. . . .

Genetically Modified Food May Render Cancer Incurable

Many substances contained only in biologically grown raw fruit and vegetables are able to induce the immune cascade against tumors, bring about detoxification and the particular phenomenon of apoptosis (suicide) of diseased cells. The explanation of the effectiveness of these vegetarian diets lies in the fact that patients do not consume food containing all the potential factors which promote cell growth, in particular they do not simultaneously consume the nine essential amino acids (Valin, Isoleucin, Leucin, Lisin, Metionin, Hystidine, Tryphtophan, Phenylalanine, Treonine), nucleic acids (DNA, RNA), vitamin B12, folic acid and also paraaminobenzoic acid [PABA]. Once, the foods which contained all of these were of animal origin (meat, fish, eggs, milk, cheese, butter); both Gerson [a nonprofit organization dedicated to nontoxic treatment of disease] and other authors (including Chinese and Indian medicine) forbade the consumption of these foods for at least a year. A vegetarian diet, based on cereals, fruit and vegetables, is, thus, the winning diet. These foods are rich in protein and their use in cancer therapy by the Gerson [Institute] and other Western, Chinese and Indian schools of natural medicine might seem surprising. No cereal and no vegetable contains the nine essential amino acids. However, if consumed together at the same meal they determine the intake of the nine amino acids. With the introduction on the market and possible contamination of all cereals, pulses and other vegetables with GMOs, many of these foods will contain ALL the essential amino acids, effectively rendering cancer NO LONGER curable by natural therapies like that of Gerson and many other authors.

Disease May Be Caused by Genetically Modified Food

The transgenic viruses with which GMOs are treated today enter into the DNA of the plant, modifying it in a way which is unknown to us. These viruses are supposed to lie dormant but there is nothing to stop them reactivating in a manner similar to the well known RNA

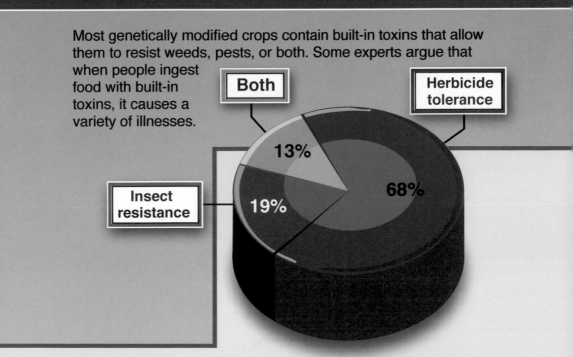

Are Genetically Modified Foods Safe to Eat?

Most genetically modified crops contain built-in toxins that allow them to resist weeds, pests, or both. Some experts argue that when people ingest food with built-in toxins, it causes a variety of illnesses.

Both

Herbicide tolerance

Insect resistance

13%

19%

68%

Taken from: Terri Raney and Pirabhu Pingali, "Sowing a Gene Revolution," *Scientific American*, September 2007, p. 106.

oncogenic viruses (Oncornavirus) or the DNA oncogenic viruses (both inducers of leukemia, sarcomas, carcinomas, gliomas). These viruses can also be the carriers of new diseases or syndromes whose dynamics are still unfortunately little understood (AIDS, Mad Cow Disease etc.), and whose origins remain very vague.

EVALUATING THE AUTHOR'S ARGUMENTS:

In this viewpoint Guiseppe Nacci uses scientific facts and examples to support his argument that genetically modified foods can cause disease in humans. He does not, however, use any quotations to support his point. If you were to rewrite this article and insert quotations, what authorities might you quote from? Where would you place these quotations to bolster the points Nacci makes?

Viewpoint

4

Genetically Modified Food Should Be Labeled

Jennifer Lapidus

"Without labeling, the consumer is unaware of the foods that are being brought to the dinner table."

In the following viewpoint Jennifer Lapidus argues that genetically modified food and products that contain GM ingredients should be labeled. Lapidus explains that the FDA, the government agency that regulates the food and drug industry, does not currently require products that contain genetically modified ingredients to be labeled. As a result, genetically modified food is unknowingly consumed by most Americans. Lapidus argues that since some evidence exists that consuming genetically modified foods is dangerous, consumers have a right to know what is in the food they eat. Until more is known about the health effects of genetically modified foods, Lapidus concludes, the government should mandate the labeling of these foods in the interest of public safety.

Lapidus is owner and operator of Natural Bridge Bakery, a wood-fired brick oven bakery that produces natural whole wheat Belgian breads.

Jennifer Lapidus, "Cloning and GMO Foods: Jennifer Lapidus Gives Us the Early 2007 Update on the Science of Our Dinner Plate," *New Life Journal*, vol. 8, March 2007, p. 18. Copyright © 2007 New Life Journal, www.newlifejournal.com. Reproduced by permission.

AS YOU READ, CONSIDER THE FOLLOWING QUESTIONS:
1. What does the author mean by "the choice is out of our hands" when she describes the lack of labeling on genetically engineered foods?
2. What two countries does the author say have no genetically modified food labeling laws?
3. How does Lapidus say shopping at a farmer's market can benefit customers who are concerned about genetically modified food?

Agricultural biotechnology has come a long way since the development of bread baking, cheese making, and the brewing of wine and beer. Today [2007], this realm equates to prolific developments in genetically modified organisms (GMOs) and cloning.

Genetically Modified Organisms Are Prevalent in the United States

Simply defined, GMOs are animals or plants whose genetic makeup, or DNA, has been altered with genetic material from another variety or species. This is different from cross-breeding, selective breeding or hybridizing of the past. This is the actual manipulation of DNA, where pigs may, for example, contain spinach genes or corn may contain the anti-freeze gene from a flounder. Cloning refers to the process of creating an identical copy of an original plant, animal or other organism; in terms of agricultural biotechnology, DNA cloning produces multiple copies of single genes or segments of DNA. Corn, soybeans and rapeseed plant (used to make canola oil) are the most prevalent GMO crops grown and consumed in the United States. Other GMOs include Bovine Growth Hormone, also known as rbGH [or BGH], which increases milk production when injected into cows and *Bacillus thuringiensis*, or Bt toxin, which is often found in potatoes. This toxin-producing gene from a bacterium called Bt is introduced to crops for purposes of creating a "built-in" pesticide rather than relying upon sprays. GMO food first appeared on grocery shelves twelve years ago. Since genetically modified soy, corn and canola are used in many processed foods, it is estimated that at least

60 to 75 percent of the foods sold in grocery stores in the United States contain genetically modified ingredients. The Food and Drug Administration [FDA] recently proposed the sale of cloned animals for meat and their milk in this country, and since it is deemed safe by the FDA, no labeling would be required.

Genetically Modified Foods Cannot Be Identified Without Labels

According to an article printed in the January 7th, 2007 issue of the *Gainesville Times,* "The FDA ruled that since BGH was considered safe, there was no need to put a label on products derived from BGH-injected cows. Without that information, shoppers had no way of avoiding such products when they went to their local supermarket. . . . The same scenario appears likely with the cloning issue. The FDA

Americans Are Wary of Genetically Modified Food

Despite the fact that more genetically modified crops are planted every year, Americans remain wary of them. A 2007 poll found that a majority of adults said they are unlikely to eat such foods. The poll also found that women are more likely than men to be suspicious of genetically modified food: 61 percent of women said they would be unlikely to eat GM foods, compared to 46 percent of men.

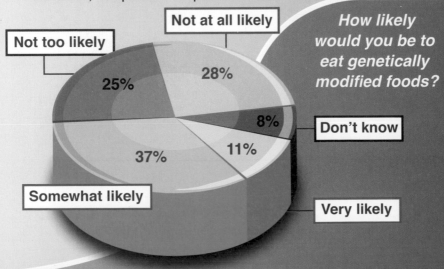

Not at all likely — 28%

Not too likely — 25%

Somewhat likely — 37%

Very likely — 11%

Don't know — 8%

How likely would you be to eat genetically modified foods?

Taken from: Pew Initiative on Agriculture and Biotechnology/Mellman Group, 2007.

says it will not require cloned products to be labeled because they are genetically and nutritionally no different from what's already on the market."

Whether genetic modification and cloning for consumption is safe is up for debate; there is an equal amount of information to support both its safety and its dangers. Yet, without labeling, the consumer is unaware of the foods that are being brought to the dinner table, so "the choice is out of our hands." It is a very different story throughout Europe and many other countries around the world, however. GMO crops are currently very rare in Europe since its consumers have demanded strict labeling laws. There are GMO-free zones throughout Europe, as well as an unofficial EU [European Union] moratorium on GMO crops. Mexico has just initiated a ban on GMO corn. In fact, the United States and Argentina remain the only two coun-

The FDA does not require cloned meat products to be labeled because they are no different genetically or nutritionally than conventional meats.

tries with no labeling laws. Although labeling genetically altered food is not required, food production is indeed regulated in the United States. For the small-scale producer, this unfortunately translates into costly regulatory procedures intended for large-scale facilities, and, in turn, often keeps quality foods from entering the marketplace. Raw milk is illegal in most states, even though producing it and its products on a small-scale is viable, accountable and highly nutritious.

FAST FACT

A Rutgers University study found that 89 percent of Americans feel that genetically modified foods should be required to have labels.

In an Op-Ed article published in the January 14th, 2007 *New York Times,* Chef Dan Barber states, "A one-size-fits-all mentality dictates that mom-and-pop slaughterhouses must follow the same rules of inspection as industrial plants, even though these huge meat processors typically slaughter more cattle in a single hour (390, Agriculture Department estimates) than their counterparts might in a whole year."

Labeling GM Food Gives Consumers a Choice

The one-size-fits-all regulatory framework makes it very difficult for the small-scale food producer to produce food profitably and with integrity. Food distribution systems favor size, so even if a food is labeled "organic," it has often traveled thousands of petroleum-induced miles. Although this picture appears bleak, there is recourse within our local communities. During farmer's market season (mid-April to November) Asheville [North Carolina] and its surrounding communities host numerous farmer's markets. Market season provides us with ample opportunity to choose between buying mass-market groceries and buying locally produced food. Shopping at a farmer's market means purchasing goods directly from the farmer or producer and bypassing the need for labeling or any distribution system. In doing so, we help create real, viable local economies, form relationships, and ensure the health of our community. It is also about making connections and bringing this largess to our dinner table. Our local farmer's market is a gem on a necklace made up of farmer's markets all over this country and abroad. Together, in the co-production of our food—both grower and consumer create an undeniable voice that can alter the course of food production in this country.

EVALUATING THE AUTHOR'S ARGUMENTS:

In this viewpoint Jennifer Lapidus argues that genetically modified food should be labeled so consumers who do not want to eat it can avoid it. Do you think the U.S. government should require labels to be put on foods that contain genetically modified ingredients? Why or why not? Explain your position using evidence from the texts you have read.

Genetically Modified Food Should Not Have to Be Labeled

Chris MacDonald and Melissa Whellams

"An agri-food company has no ethical obligation to label its GM foods."

In the following viewpoint Chris MacDonald and Melissa Whellams argue that genetically modified ingredients should not have to be identified on food labels. Currently, North American governments do not require companies to label genetically modified ingredients, which are in many packaged foods. The authors explain that tests have found genetically modified food to be just as safe as traditional food. Since these foods do not threaten human health, the authors see little need to mandate food manufacturers to label products that contain genetically engineered ingredients. Furthermore, the authors claim that many consumers would be confused by such a label and would have difficulty understanding what the term "genetically

Chris MacDonald and Melissa Whellams, "Corporate Decisions About Labelling Genetically Modified Foods," *Journal of Business Ethics*, vol. 75, October 2007, pp. 187–90. Copyright © 2007 Springer Science and Business Media. With kind permission from Springer Science and Business Media, conveyed through Copyright Clearance Center, and authors.

modified" even means. For these reasons, they conclude that until there is proof that labeling genetically modified food would protect consumers, there is no reason to mandate it.

MacDonald is associate professor in the Philosophy Department at Saint Mary's University in Halifax, Nova Scotia. He is president of the Canadian Society for the Study of Practical Ethics and a member of the editorial board of the *Journal of Business Ethics*. Whellams works at Canadian Business for Social Responsibility (CBSR) as a corporate social responsibility (CSR) adviser for the extractive industries.

AS YOU READ, CONSIDER THE FOLLOWING QUESTIONS:
1. What percentage of food in grocery stores do the authors say contains genetically modified ingredients?
2. According to MacDonald and Whellams, how might the labeling of some genetically modified food negatively impact a company's business?
3. Genetically modified foods have been deemed to be safe for human consumption by what major organization, according to the authors?

Background: The GM Food Labelling Debate

There has been considerable discussion, over the last few years, of whether and how agri-food companies should convey to consumers information regarding various characteristics of their products. Not surprisingly (given the special attention paid these days to all things bearing the word "genetic") one topic that has been a particular focus of attention by the public, the media, and academics has been the issue of labelling GM foods.

Genetic modification in principle refers to "any change to the heritable traits of an organism achieved by intentional manipulation" (Health Canada, 2003). By definition this includes traditional cross-breeding techniques, although the recent frenzy over GM foods pertains primarily to transgenic modification achieved through micro-manipulation of genetic material in laboratories.

Since 1994, Health Canada (the federal agency responsible for food safety) has approved the sale of over 60 "novel foods" in Canada, including genetically modified corn, soybeans, potatoes, canola, and squash (Health Canada, 2004). As soy and corn derivatives such as soy flour, soy protein, corn meal, corn syrup, soy oil, and corn oil are common ingredients in packaged foods, it is safe to say that—whether they know it or not—most Canadians have consumed GM foods or products containing GM ingredients. According to Food and Consumer Products Manufacturers of Canada (FCPMC), 60–70% of food products on grocery shelves contain GM ingredients (National Institute of Nutrition, 2001).

By the late 1990s, there was relatively high consumer awareness about GM foods in Canada. An Angus Reid poll conducted in the fall of 1999 reported that 78% of Canadians surveyed had seen, read, or heard something about GM foods. Thirty-two percent of those surveyed identified "food safety/health concerns/allergies" as a risk associated with GM foods (Ag-West Biotech Inc., 2000). According to an Ipsos-Reid/Globe and Mail poll conducted in August of 2001, 63% of Canadians stated that they would be less likely to buy food that had been genetically modified or contained genetically modified ingredients (Foss, 2001). In a (mostly) free market where consumers can voice their opinions with their dollars, one might wonder how GM products have managed to stay on the shelves. However, GM foods fall into the category of "credence goods", products that have certain characteristics that are not apparent to consumers before or even after consumption. Thus consumers so far have had no way of identifying whether particular foods were a product of genetic modification. . . .

Dilema for the Individual Company

The situation faced by individual agri-food companies, then, is one in which they know that the public has—whether for good or bad reasons—considerable misgivings about GM foods, but in which neither the market nor the government has responded to those misgivings. We thus have the makings of a "hard problem" of ethics. That is, companies are faced with a situation in which they are arguably being dishonest with their customers (committing a lie of omission), but in which a unilateral change in strategy (positive-labelling of their GM products, when no one else is doing so) would almost certainly have a significant deleterious effect on market share. Many public advocacy groups, and at least some scholars, have advocated for labelling as an ethical requirement. Jackson, for example, argues that labelling "fosters consumer autonomy and moves toward more participatory decision-making."

Given this characterization of the issue, what's a well-intentioned company to do? Should it voluntarily label its GM products or not? Do individual corporations have an ethical obligation to act, in the face of a failure of key democratic institutions to give the public what it wants?

At least some companies have taken this on as an ethical obligation. The website for an American company called AquaBounty—producer of a fast-growing, genetically modified strain of salmon—

Proponents of not labeling of GM products say agri-food companies have no ethical obligation to label their products.

states that the company "has made a company decision to require that all licensees growing AquAdvantage fish agree to a labelling requirement." So apparently at least some companies seem to agree with activist organizations in feeling that it is ethically incumbent upon agri-food companies to engage in positive-labelling of their GM products.

We argue, however, that although unilateral action in this regard might be admirable, an agri-food company has no ethical obligation to label its GM foods, given the current social, legal, scientific, and economic context. While neither government complacency nor market failure constitutes a general excuse for inaction on the part of individual corporations, we argue that the particular characteristics of this case make it unreasonable to expect unilateral action. . . .

No Legal Standard, and No Expression of Concern by Government

To date, North American governments have declined to require labelling of GM foods. There is thus no legal requirement for companies to indicate, through labelling or any other means, that their food products either are genetically modified, or contain genetically modified ingredients. Of course, those of us who teach ethics are often at pains to point out that law and ethics are two separate domains. Thus the fact that companies that fail to label their GM foods are breaking no laws does not immediately imply that they are doing nothing unethical. Yet here we argue that in highly regulated industries such as food, agriculture, and biotechnology, the absence of specific regulation does provide an important piece of evidence to be used in the determination of the ethical status of a given piece of corporate behaviour. . . .

Further, note that far from there being any legal requirement regarding GM food labelling, there has not even been any official

> **FAST FACT**
>
> The United States does not currently have any laws that state foods containing genetically modified organisms must be labeled as such.

expressions of *concern* by North American regulatory agencies. If there were such expressions of concern—for example, by Health Canada or the U.S. Food and Drug Administration—this might signal that regulatory action was in the offing. In such circumstances, we might think it ethically appropriate for companies to be proactive, rather than waiting to be legally forced to act. But far from expressing concern, Health Canada has declared GM foods to be just as safe as non-GM foods. And a spokesman for the FDA has declared: "we have seen no evidence that the bioengineered foods now on the market pose any human health concerns or that they are in any way less safe than crops produced through traditional breeding."

No Well-documented Danger to Human Health

Even in the absence of legal or regulatory action by government, agri-food companies might well be ethically required to take action if there were credible, non-speculative evidence that the products they were selling posed a threat to human health. Companies have a positive obligation to act when the health of consumers is at stake. So, for example, we generally see it as ethically mandatory for pharmaceutical or medical devices companies who become aware of dangers posed by their products to recall those products, even in advance of action by regulators. The Dow Corning breast implant debacle is a well-known example of a company's failure in this regard. And Johnson & Johnson's handling of the Tylenol crisis is a classic example of a company acting admirably in this regard. The general principle, here, is that if a company's product is hurting people, and if it is possible to eliminate or mitigate that harm, then a company is ethically required to do so.

A review of the extensive literature debating the safety of GM foods is beyond the scope of this paper. But our reading of the meta-analyses offered by various blue-ribbon panels suggests that to date, no substantive risk has been detected. According to the World Health Organization, "GM foods currently available on the international market have passed risk assessments and are not likely to present risks for human health." . . .

Genetically Engineered Ingredients Are in Many Common Foods

Federal law does not currently require genetically modified ingredients to be labeled on packaging, but such ingredients are found in many common products, including most commercial brands of cereal, salsa, snack foods, cookies, and other food. The following is a list of various cracker brands that use non–genetically and genetically engineered ingredients.

Non–Genetically Engineered Ingredients	Genetically Engineered Ingredients
Appeteasers (Adrienne's) Cheddar, Double Cheddar, Garlic and Herb	**Keebler (Keebler/Flowers Industries)** Town House Club Munch 'Ems (all varieties), Wheatables, Zesta Saltines, Toasteds (Wheat, Onion, Sesame & Butter Crisps), Snax Stix (Wheat, Cheddar & Original), Harvest Bakery (Multigrain, Butter, Corn Bread)
Barbara's Bakery Wheatines, Sesame Wheatines, Cracked Pepper Wheatines, Salted Top Wheatines	
Courtneys (Adrienne's) Classic Flavor, Savoury Herbs, Cracked Pepper, Sun-Dried Tomato	**Nabisco (Nabisco/Philip Morris)** Ritz (all varieties), Wheat Thins (all), Wheatsworth, Triscuits
Darcia's Crostini (Adrienne's) Original, Rosemary, Onion, Fennel	
Ener-G Foods Hol-Grain Snack Thins, Hol Grain Onion & Garlic, Melba Toast	**Waverly** Sociables, Better Cheddars, Premium Saltines (all), Ritz Snack Mix (all), Vegetable Flavor Crisps, Swiss Cheese Flavor Crisps, Cheese Nips (all), Uneeda Biscuits
Hain Wheatettes, Rich Crackers, Sesame Wheat	
Lavosh-Hawaii (Adrienne's) Classic Island Crackers, Caraway Rye Crackers, Slightly Onion Crackers, Peppercorn Crackers, Rosemary & Garlic Crackers, Ten-Grain Crackers, Mini-Bite Snack Crackers	**Pepperidge Farm (Campbell's)** Butter Thins, Hearty Wheat Cracker Trio, Cracker Quartet, Three Cheese Snack Stix, Sesame Snack Stix, Pumpernickel Snack Stix, Goldfish (original, cheddar, parmesan, pizza, pretzel), Goldfish Snack Mix (all)
Wasa (Novartis) Whole Wheat with Oats, Fruit Cinnamon Toast	**Red Oval Farms (Nabisco/ Philip Morris)** Stoned Wheat Thins (all varieties), Crisp 'N Light Sourdough Rye, Crisp 'N Light Wheat
Whole Foods Water Crackers, Cracked Pepper Water Crackers, Woven Wheats	
Wild Oats Stone Ground Wheat, Wheat Weavers Water Crackers, Wheat Weavers Veggie Herb, Stone Ground Wheat	**Sunshine (Flowers Industries)** Cheez-It (original & reduced fat), Cheez-It White Cheddar, Cheez-It Party Mix, Krispy Original Saltines

No Clear Right to Know

Among the most persuasive arguments in favour of labelling GM foods has been the claim that, independent of concrete evidence about risk, consumers have a *right* to know what they are eating. For many consumers, labelling is not about risk, but about freedom, autonomy, and informed control. The key moral claim, here, is that "I have a right to know what I'm eating." . . .

Before we get too serious about attributing a right, on the part of consumers, to know whether their food is genetically modified, we ought to ask whether unilateral labelling by individual companies is an effective means of fulfilling the interests that such a right would seek to protect. That is, even if we agree that (at least some) consumers have a serious interest in knowing whether their foods are genetically modified, such that having that knowledge would contribute significantly to their well-being, it is not at all clear that unilateral action by individual companies (the topic of this paper) would be the best way to satisfy that interest. For one thing, there are serious concerns about whether consumers in general will know what a particular label ("GM-Free", or "May contain some genetically engineered ingredients") actually means. Further, if some, but not all companies engage in labelling (some in positive-labelling, some in negative labelling), will consumers really have enough information about the range of products available to them to make informed, effective choices about the things that matter to them?

Thus many significant challenges remain, many obstacles to taking seriously the idea that consumers have a right to know whether their food is genetically modified, a right that would impose upon various companies a correlative obligation to label their foods. For the time being, then, it is impossible to take such a rights claim seriously.

Conclusion

We conclude, then, that at the current time the issue of labelling GM foods has none of the key characteristics that, if present, might well make such labelling ethically mandatory for individual agri-food companies. The argument presented here does not necessarily imply that governments ought not to require labelling, or that the agri-food industry ought not be more responsive to consumers' concerns. We simply argue that given the lack of government intervention, the lack of collective action on the part of the industry, and the lack of clear evidence of risk to human health, individual companies cannot reasonably be expected to take unilateral action.

EVALUATING THE AUTHORS' ARGUMENTS:

In this viewpoint MacDonald and Whellams argue it is unnecessary to label products that contain genetically modified food. How do you think the author of the preceding viewpoint, Jennifer Lapidus, might respond to this argument? Explain your answer using evidence from the texts.

The Government Should Regulate Genetically Modified Food

Dennis J. Kucinich

"Congress must provide a comprehensive regulatory framework for all genetically engineered products."

Dennis J. Kucinich is a Democratic member of the U.S. House of Representatives for Ohio's Tenth District. In the following viewpoint he argues that the government needs to regulate the genetically modified food industry to ensure the safety of the American people. Current food and safety laws are outdated and do not take into account the recent advances in food technology, Kucinich explains. Therefore, he says the government needs to design a framework for regulating these new products. Kucinich thinks regulations should include policies that require the labeling of all food that contains genetically modified ingredients; the institution of a review process of engineered foods; protections to farmers who produce traditional crops; making biotechnology companies responsible for any problems associated with the foods they create; and monitoring the pharmaceutical and industrial crop industry to

Dennis J. Kucinich, "Introduction of Genetically Engineered Regulatory Framework," in Congressional Record–Extensions of Remarks, May 2, 2006.

avoid contamination of food crops. Kucinich concludes that these regulations will ensure that the benefits of genetically modified foods are maximized and that the potential hazards are reduced.

Kucinich was a candidate for the Democratic nomination for president of the United States in the 2004 and 2008 elections. He currently serves as chairman of the Domestic Policy Subcommittee of the House Committee on Oversight and Government Reform.

AS YOU READ, CONSIDER THE FOLLOWING QUESTIONS:
1. According to Kucinich, what do Americans have the right to know about their food?
2. What role should the Food and Drug Administration play in regulating genetically engineered foods, according to the author?
3. What are pharmaceutical and industrial crops, and what does the author say can prevent them from contaminating food crops?

"Mr. Speaker, I rise in support of six bills I introduced today that will provide a comprehensive regulatory framework for all genetically engineered plants, animals, bacteria, and other organisms. The bills will protect our food, environment, and health. They are a common-sense precaution to ensure genetically engineered foods do no harm.

"Genetic engineering is having a serious impact on the food we eat, on the environment, and on farmers. To ensure we can maximize benefits and minimize hazards, Congress must provide a comprehensive regulatory framework for all genetically engineered products.

"Current laws, such as our food safety and environmental laws, were not written with this technology in mind. Clearer laws are necessary to ensure that these new scientific capabilities and the associated impacts are closely monitored.

"The six bills include the Genetically Engineered Food Right to Know Act of 2006, which requires food companies to label all foods that contain or are produced with genetically engineered materials and instructs the Food and Drug Administration [FDA] to conduct periodic tests to ensure compliance. This is a basic consumer rights and consumer safety issue. People have a right to know what is in the food they are eating, and that the food is safe.

"Combined, these bills would ensure that consumers are protected, increase food safety, protect farmer rights, make biotech companies liable for their products, and help developing nations resolve hunger concerns."

Summary of Genetically Engineered Food Legislation

Consumers wish to know whether the food they purchase and consume is a genetically engineered food. Concerns include the potential transfer of allergens into food and other health risks, potential environmental risks associated with the genetic engineering of crops, and religiously and ethically based dietary restrictions. Adoption and implementation of mandatory labeling requirements for genetically engineered food produced in the United States would facilitate international trade. It would allow American farmers and companies to export and appropriately market their products—both genetically engineered and non–genetically engineered—to foreign customers. This bill acknowledges consumers have a right to know what genetically engineered foods they are eating:

- Requires food companies to label all foods that contain or are produced with genetically engineered material and requires the FDA to periodically test products to ensure compliance.
- Voluntary, non-GE food labels are authorized.
- A legal framework is established to ensure the accuracy of labeling without creating significant economic hardship on the food production system.

The Genetically Engineered Food Safety Act

Given the consensus among the scientific community that genetic engineering can potentially introduce hazards, such as allergens or toxins, genetically engineered foods need to be evaluated on a case-by-case basis and cannot be presumed to be generally recognized as safe. The possibility of such hazards dictates a cautious approach to genetically engineered food approvals. However, FDA has glossed over the food safety concerns of genetically engineered foods and not taken steps to ensure the safety of these genetically engineered foods. This bill requires that all genetically engineered foods follow a strenuous food safety review process:

- Requires FDA to screen all genetically engineered foods through the current food additive process to ensure they are safe for human consumption, yet continues FDA discretion in applying the safety factors that are generally recognized as appropriate.
- Requires that unique concerns be explicitly examined in the review process, a phase out of antibiotic resistance markers, and a prohibition on known allergens.
- Requires the FDA to conduct a public comment period of at least 30 days.

The Genetically Engineered Crop and Animal Farmer Protection Act

Agribusiness and biotechnology companies have rapidly consolidated market power at the same time as the average farmer's profits and viability have significantly declined. Policies promoted by biotech corporations have systematically acted to remove basic farmer rights enjoyed since the beginning of agriculture. These policies include unreasonable seed contracts, the intrusion into everyday farm operations, and liability burdens. The introduction of genetically engineered crops has also created obstacles for farmers, including the loss of markets and increased liability concerns. To mitigate the abuses upon farmers, a clear set of farmer rights must be established. This bill provides several farmer rights and protections to maintain the opportunity to farm:

> **FAST FACT**
>
> The "Genetically Engineered Food Right to Know Act of 1999" was first introduced into the U.S. Congress by Dennis Kucinich in 1999. Since then, numerous pieces of legislation have been introduced into Congress.

- Farmers may save seeds and seek compensation for failed genetically engineered crops.
- Biotech companies may not: shift liability to farmers; nor require access to farmer's property; nor mandate arbitration; nor mandate

court of jurisdiction; nor require damages beyond actual fees; nor charge more to American farmers for use of this technology, than they charge farmers in other nations, or any other unfair condition.

- Seed companies must: ensure seeds labeled non-GE are accurate; provide clear instructions to reduce cross-pollination, which contaminates other fields; and inform farmers of the risks of using genetically engineered crops.
- The EPA is required to evaluate the concern of Bt resistant pests and take actions necessary to prevent resistance to Bt, an important organic pesticide.
- The bill prohibits genetic engineering designed to produce sterile seeds and loan discrimination based on the choice of seeds an agricultural producer uses.

The Genetically Engineered Organism Liability Act

Biotech companies are selling a technology that is being commercialized far in advance of the new and unknown science of genetic engineering. Farmers may suffer from crop failures, neighboring farmers may suffer from cross pollination, increased insect resistance, and unwanted 'volunteer' genetically engineered plants, and consumers may suffer from health and environmental impacts. Therefore, biotech companies should be found liable for the failures of genetically engineered crops. This bill ensures that the creator of the technology assumes all liability:

- The bill places all liability from negative impacts of genetically engineered organisms squarely upon the biotechnology companies that created the genetically engineered organism.
- Farmers are granted indemnification to protect them from the liabilities of biotech companies.
- The bill prohibits any transfer of liability away from the biotechnology companies that created the genetically engineered organism.

Real Solutions to World Hunger Act

The demand for mandatory labeling, safety testing, and farmer protections do not constitute obstacles to the cessation of world hunger. Economics remain the significant barrier to a consistent food supply,

In May of 2006 Ohio congressional representative Dennis Kucinich introduced bills in Congress to regulate the genetically modified food industry.

and the development of expensive genetically engineered foods may only exacerbate this trend. Almost all research funding for the development of genetically engineered food targets the developed nation's agriculture and consumers. However, agroecological interventions have had significantly more success in helping developing nations feed themselves with higher yields and improved environmental practices, all within reasonable costs for developing countries. This bill offers several new initiatives and protections to help developing nations resolve their hunger concerns:

- To protect developing nations, genetically engineered exports are restricted to those already approved in the U.S. and approved by the importing nation.
- The bill creates an international research fund for sustainable agriculture research paid for by the Sustainable Agriculture Trust Fund, a small tax on biotechnology company profits.

The Genetically Engineered Pharmaceutical and Industrial Crop Safety Act

A pharmaceutical crop or industrial crop is a plant that has been genetically engineered to produce a medical or industrial product, including human and veterinary drugs. Many of the novel substances produced in pharmaceutical crops and industrial crops are for particular medical or industrial purposes only. These substances are not intended to be incorporated in food or to be spread into the environment. That would be equivalent to allowing a prescription drug in the food supply. Experts acknowledge that contamination of human food and animal feed is inevitable due to the inherent imprecision of biological and agricultural systems. This contamination by pharmaceutical crops and industrial crops poses substantial liability and other economic risks to farmers, grain handlers, and food companies. This bill attempts to prevent contamination of our food supply by pharmaceutical crops and industrial crops:

- The bill places a temporary moratorium on pharmaceutical crops and industrial crops until all regulations required in this bill are in effect.
- The bill places a permanent moratorium on pharmaceutical crops and industrial crops grown in an open-air environment and on pharmaceutical crops and industrial crops grown in a commonly used food source.
- The United States Department of Agriculture shall establish a tracking system to regulate the growing, handling, transportation, and disposal of all pharmaceutical and industrial crops and their by products to prevent contamination.

- The National Academy of Sciences shall submit to Congress a report that explores alternative methods to produce pharmaceuticals or industrial chemicals that have the advantage of being conducted in controlled production facilities and do not present the risk of contamination.

EVALUATING THE AUTHOR'S ARGUMENTS:

In this viewpoint Kucinich describes six ways the government should regulate the genetically modified food industry. Of all those discussed, which regulation do you think would be the most effective in protecting the public from the potential dangers of genetically modified food? Why? Explain your answer using evidence from the texts.

Chapter 2

Can Genetically Modified Food Alleviate World Hunger?

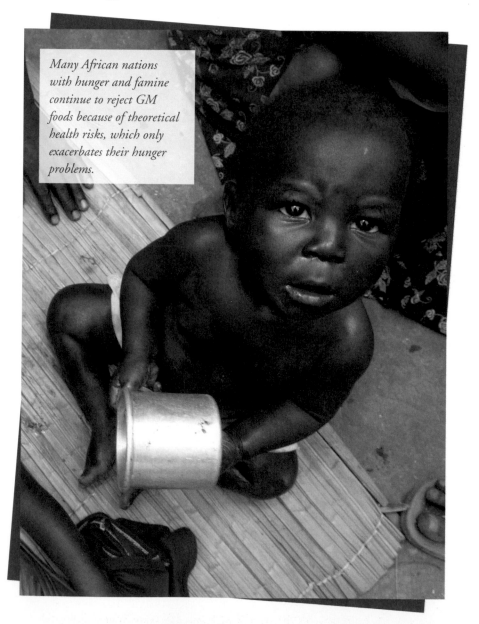

Many African nations with hunger and famine continue to reject GM foods because of theoretical health risks, which only exacerbates their hunger problems.

Genetically Modified Food Can Eliminate Hunger

Temba Nolutshungu

"GM products . . . are just the tools that we need to boost exports and fight famine."

In the following viewpoint Temba Nolutshungu argues that genetically modified food can help alleviate world hunger. Millions of people are starving around the world, particularly in African nations like Zambia, Uganda, and Kenya. Nolutshungu suggests solving the problem with genetically modified crops, which he says are inexpensive and reliable. Nolutshungu laments that many hungry countries have banned genetically modified food despite the fact that it seems to offer relief from hunger. He urges governments not to irrationally fear engineered food but to welcome it as a source of nourishment and plenty for their people. By not accepting the food technology that has proven successful in Canada and America, Nolutshungu concludes that the cycle of famine is needlessly perpetuated around the world.

Temba Nolutshungu, "GM Food and the Harm of Hysteria," *Business Day*, February 19, 2007. Copyright © 2004 BDFM Publishers (Pty) Ltd. All rights reserved. Reproduced by permission.

Nolutshungu is a director of the Free Market Foundation, an independent policy research and education organization founded in 1975 to promote the principles of limited government, economic freedom, and individual liberty in southern Africa.

AS YOU READ, CONSIDER THE FOLLOWING QUESTIONS:
1. How long does Nolutshungu say Americans and Canadians have been safely eating genetically modified foods?
2. What is the "precautionary principle," and how is it being used to hurt hungry people, according to the author?
3. What two reasons does the author give for why famine-stricken African countries have not fully embraced genetically modified foods?

European consumer panic and European Union (EU) regulations about genetically modified (GM) foods threaten millions of starving Africans, who need cheap and reliable crops. Greenpeace has just garnered a million signatures around Europe for a petition to the EU demanding labels for traces of GM organisms in food. This time last year, Zambia banned famine relief containing GM food. Uganda and Kenya are wavering and millions of people are starving in Africa right now. GM food may not solve malnutrition and starvation by itself, but it would make a huge difference.

Genetically Modified Foods Are Safe

Remember, we are talking about a product that has been eaten by Americans and Canadians for more than a decade without harming anybody: even the EU, while applying many restrictions, accepts that it is safer than conventional food.

Fifteen years of tests in 400 European laboratories led EU research commissioner Philippe Busquin to say in 2001 that they had not found "any new risks to human health or the environment, beyond the usual uncertainties of conventional plant breeding".

"Indeed, the use of more precise technology and the greater regulatory scrutiny probably make them even safer than conventional plants and foods," Busquin said.

Irrational Fears About GM Foods Hurt Starving People

Even SA [South Africa], with bumper harvests of GM crops, is threatened by irrational fears, with activists calling for restrictive laws, citing the "precautionary principle"—a legal concept that is promoted by the EU and the United Nations.

Can Genetically Modified Crops Feed the World?

Hunger is a global problem—the United States estimates that one child dies from hunger and related causes every five seconds. In parts of Africa and Asia, as much as 35 percent of the population is starving. Crops that are engineered to withstand tough growing conditions and pests could offer hope to millions of hungry people.

Percent of population undernourished

| | no data | | 2.5% | | 2.5–4% | | 5–19% | | 20–34% | | 35% |

Eastern Europe & Baltic States

North America & the Caribbean

Commonwealth of Independent States

Near Asia

East Asia

North Africa

South Asia

West Africa

Central America

South America

Central Africa

East Africa

Southeast Asia & Oceania

Southern Africa

Hunger in the Developing World

Total Population	4,712,200,000
Total Undernourished	797,900,000
% of total Population	16%

Taken from: United Nations World Food Programme.

At first sight, the precautionary principle looks reasonable. As children, we were warned that you should "look before you leap" or told that "if in doubt, don't".

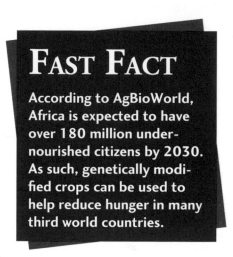

FAST FACT

According to AgBioWorld, Africa is expected to have over 180 million undernourished citizens by 2030. As such, genetically modified crops can be used to help reduce hunger in many third world countries.

Following that advice will at times have avoided danger, loss and even injury. On the other hand, following precautionary advice to avoid all risk would keep away a lot of fine opportunities, and carrying out a risk assessment before avoiding an oncoming bus could prove fatal.

The precautionary principle requires action to avoid a risk even when there is no evidence of any risk: it demands that new inventions should not be used unless and until they have been shown to be absolutely safe, reversing the usual burden of proof: they are assumed to be harmful until proven safe to an impossible standard.

When the Zambian government turned away famine-relief GM maize in 2005 because of a theoretical health risk, it created a real risk and turned a disaster into a tragedy. But that same type of GM maize had been consumed by Americans and Canadians for more than a decade.

Genetically Modified Foods Reduce Hunger

Applied to agriculture and food biotechnology, the precautionary principle ignores the real threats of hunger, starvation and malnutrition that can be reduced by new products. Applied to penicillin and aspirin or peanuts and potatoes, with rare fatal allergies, it would have demanded an outright ban.

Yet GM foods do not even have those rare side effects. It is worth repeating that no one has yet detected any allergy, harm or risk to humans, animals or the environment from commercialised GM crops.

Farmers use GM seeds because they are more efficient, giving higher yields and lower pesticide costs. Consumers eat GM foods because they are just as good as any other crop, and cheaper too. Hundreds of millions of people, rich and poor, get income or food from them.

The "Frankenfood" myths about terminator genes, contamination and the destruction of species reflect only ignorance, pseudoscience or plain propaganda.

Europeans march in protest against GM foods in Brussels, Belgium, even though Americans and Canadians have been consuming GM foods for over ten years with no ill effects.

GM Foods Can Fight Famine

In a continent that desperately needs growth, foods, jobs and exports, innovation is exactly what we need.

The US, Canada and Argentina had the muscle to bring their GM-export case to the World Trade Organisation and to win against the EU last year, but African countries are still vulnerable to EU restrictions on GM products and consumer fears of (unspecified) contamination.

Bizarrely, those barriers are supported by western activists in the aid industry, who are all opposed to free trade and GM products, ignoring the fact that these are just the tools that we need to boost exports and fight famine.

For European consumers, GM is a whimsical lifestyle issue. But for the poor of the world, this really is a question of life and death.

EVALUATING THE AUTHOR'S ARGUMENTS:

Temba Nolutshungu argues that banning genetically modified food hurts starving people more than consuming such food would. Clarify what he means by this. Do you think he is right? Explain your answer thoroughly.

Genetically Modified Food Cannot Eliminate Hunger

Sean McDonagh

"Those who wish to banish hunger should address the social and economic inequalities that create poverty and not claim that a magic-bullet technology will solve all the problems."

In the following viewpoint Sean McDonagh argues that genetically modified food cannot alleviate world hunger. McDonagh acknowledges that hunger is a serious problem—he describes how millions of people live in famine-stricken regions and go without food on a daily basis. But genetically modified crops are not the answer to famine and hunger, in McDonagh's opinion, because they negatively impact farmland and actually reduce crop yields. As a result, hungry people end up having less food and hurt their land's ability to produce more. McDonagh says conventional crops are a better food source than genetically modified crops, but the best long-term solution to hunger is to remedy its real causes: economic inequality and lack of access to farming tools. These issues cannot be addressed with genetically modified food, the author concludes.

Sean McDonagh, "Genetic Engineering Is Not the Answer," *America*, vol. 192, May 2, 2005, pp. 8–10.
Copyright © 2005 www.americamagazine.org. All rights reserved. Reproduced by permission of America Press. For subscription information, visit www.americamagazine.org.

McDonagh is a Catholic priest who spent many years as a missionary in the Philippines. He is the author of several books on ecology and religion, including *The Death of Life: The Horror of Extinction.*

AS YOU READ, CONSIDER THE FOLLOWING QUESTIONS:
1. What is "terminator technology," and how does it hurt farmers who use genetically modified seeds, according to the author?
2. According to McDonagh, how does the yield from conventional breeding of sweet potatoes compare to the yield of genetically modified sweet potatoes?
3. How is Brazil proof of the idea that genetically modified food cannot relieve hunger, as reported by the author?

I n 1992 the then-chief executive of Monsanto [a biotechnology firm], Robert Shapiro, told *Harvard Business Review* that genetically modified crops will be necessary to feed a growing world population. He predicted that if population levels were to rise to 10 billion, humanity would face two options: either open up new land for cultivation or increase crop yields. Since the first choice was not feasible, because we were already cultivating marginal land and in the process creating unprecedented levels of soil erosion, we would have to choose genetic engineering. This option, Shapiro argued, was merely a further improvement on the agricultural technologies that gave rise to the Green Revolution that saved Asia from food shortages in the 1960's and 1970's.

Genetically engineered crops might seem an ideal solution. Yet both current data and past examples show problems and provoke doubts as to their necessity.

Genetic Engineering Hurts the Environment

The Green Revolution involved the production of hybrid seeds by crossing two genetically distant parents, which produced an offspring plant that gave increased yield. Critics of genetic engineering question the accepted wisdom that its impact has been entirely positive. Hybrid seeds are expensive and heavily reliant on fertilizers and pesticides. And because they lose their vigor after the first planting, the farmer must purchase new seeds for each successive planting.

In his book *Geopolitics and the Green Revolution*, John H. Perkins describes the environmentally destructive and socially unjust aspects of the Green Revolution. One of its most important negative effects, he says, is that it has contributed to the loss of three-quarters of the genetic diversity of major food crops and that the rate of erosion continues at close to 2 percent per year. The fundamental importance of genetic diversity is illustrated by the fact that when a virulent fungus began to destroy wheat fields in the United States and Canada in 1950, plant breeders staved off disaster by cross-breeding five Mexican wheat varieties with 12 imported ones. In the process they created a new strain that was able to resist so-called "stem rust." The loss of these varieties would have been a catastrophe for wheat production globally.

Genetically Engineered Seeds Threaten Subsistence Farming

The development by a Monsanto-owned company of what is benignly called a Technology Protection System—a more apt name is terminator technology—is another reason for asserting that the feed-the-world argument is completely spurious. Genetically engineered seeds that contain the terminator gene self-destruct after the first crop. Once again, this forces farmers to return to the seed companies at the beginning of each planting season. If this technology becomes widely used, it will harm the two billion subsistence farmers who live mainly in the poor countries of the world. Sharing seeds among farmers has been at the very heart of subsistence farming since the domestication of staple food crops 11,000 years ago. The terminator technology will lock farmers into a regime of buying genetically engineered seeds that are herbicide tolerant and insect resistant, tethering them to the chemical treadmill.

FAST FACT

According to Greenpeace, millions of tons of genetically engineered soybeans are exported every year from Argentina for cattle feed, while millions of Argentineans go hungry.

On an ethical level, a technology that, according to Professor Richard Lewontin of Harvard University, "introduces a 'killer' transgene that prevents the germ of the harvested grain from developing" must be considered grossly immoral. It is a sin against the poor, against previous generations who freely shared their knowledge of plant life with us, against nature itself and finally against the God of all creativity. To set out deliberately to create seeds that self-destruct is an abomination no civilized society should tolerate. Furthermore, there is danger that the terminator genes could spread to neighboring crops and to the wild and weedy relatives of the plant that has been engineered to commit suicide. This would jeopardize the food security of many poor people. . . .

False Claims Have Been Made About the Effectiveness of Genetically Modified Foods

Early in 2003 a researcher at the Institute of Development Studies at Sussex University in England published an analysis of the G.M.O.

A Monsanto employee tests GM seeds with the "terminator" gene at the Monsanto research library in Les Landes, France.

[genetically modified organisms] crops that biotech companies are developing for Africa. Among the plants studied were cotton, maize and the sweet potato. The G.M.O. research on the sweet potato is now approaching its 12th year and has involved the work of 19 scientists; to date it has cost $6 million. Results indicated that yield has increased by 18 percent. On the other hand, conventional sweet potato breeding, working with a small budget, has produced a virus-resistant variety with a 100 percent yield increase.

Claims that G.M.O.'s lead to fewer chemicals in agriculture are also being challenged. A comprehensive study using U.S. government data on the use of chemicals on genetically engineered crops was carried out by Charles Benbrook, head of the Northwest Science and Environmental Policy Center in Sandpoint, Idaho. He found that when G.M.O.'s were first introduced, they needed 25 percent fewer chemicals for the first three years. But in 2001, 5 percent more chemicals were sprayed compared with conventional crop varieties. Dr. Benbrook stated: "The proponents of biotechnology claim G.M.O. varieties substantially reduce pesticide use. While true in the first few years of widespread planting, it is not the case now. There's now clear evidence that the average pound of herbicide applied per acre planted to herbicide-tolerant varieties have increased compared to the first few years."

Genetically Modified Crops Are Not the Answer to World Hunger

Hunger and famine around the world have more to do with the absence of land reform, social inequality, bias against women farmers and the scarcity of cheap credit and basic agricultural tools than with lack of agribusiness super-seeds. This fact was recognized by those who attended the World Food Summit in Rome in November 1996. People are hungry because they do not have access to food production processes or the money to buy food. Brazil, for example, is the third largest exporter of food in the world, yet one-fifth of its population, over 30 million people, do not have enough food to eat. Clearly hunger there is not due to lack of food but to the unequal distribution of wealth and the fact that a huge number of people are landless.

Do the proponents of genetically engineered food think that agribusiness companies will distribute such food free to the hungry poor who have no money? There was food in Ireland during the famine in the 1840's, for example, but those who were starving had no access to it or money to buy it.

As a Columban missionary in the Philippines, I saw something similar during the drought caused by El Niño in 1983. There was a severe food shortage among the tribal people in the highlands of Mindanao. The drought destroyed their cereal crops, and they could no longer harvest food in the tropical forest because it had been cleared during the previous decades. Even during the height of the drought, an agribusiness corporation was exporting tropical fruit from the lowlands. There was also sufficient rice and corn in the lowlands, but the tribal people did not have the money to buy it. Had it not been for food aid from nongovernmental organizations, many of the tribal people would have starved. . . .

Those who wish to banish hunger should address the social and economic inequalities that create poverty and not claim that a magic-bullet technology will solve all the problems.

EVALUATING THE AUTHORS' ARGUMENTS:

The author of this viewpoint is a Catholic priest and former missionary. The author of the previous viewpoint, Temba Nolutshungu, is the director of the Free Market Foundation, which promotes economic freedom in southern Africa. Does knowing the background of these authors influence your opinion of their arguments? How might their experiences have affected their different positions on genetically modified food and hunger?

Genetically Modified Food Can Increase the World's Food Supply

Daniel Charles

"The technology is such a powerful tool for solving problems . . . that it has to be accepted."

In the following viewpoint Daniel Charles argues that genetically modified crops can increase the world's food supply. He explains that genetically engineered seeds have a better chance of resisting disease and can allow even the poorest farmers to raise superior varieties of corn in greater quantities. Political opposition can get in the way of advancements in biotechnology, but Charles believes that producing biotech crops that feed the poor and improve the lives of farmers in the developing world will help change the minds of opponents. Daniel Charles is an independent writer and radio producer who contributes regularly to National Public Radio's technology coverage and to *Technology Review*. He is the author of *Lords of the Harvest: Biotech, Big Money, and the Future of Food*.

Daniel Charles, "Corn That Clones Itself," *Technology Review*, March 2003. Copyright © 2003 by the Association of Alumni and Alumnae of MIT. Reproduced by permission.

AS YOU READ, CONSIDER THE FOLLOWING QUESTIONS:
1. What are some of the impacts the author lists of self-cloning plants?
2. What is apomixis and what are some of its potential benefits?
3. Name at least five other countries that are joining in on research for corn apomixis.

An hour outside of Mexico City, the taxi turns off the main road, and the noise and bustle of the highway fade away. Past a steel gate and a white guardhouse, we enter the well-tended grounds of the International Center for the Improvement of Maize and Wheat, known by its Spanish acronym, CIMMYT (pronounced SIM-it). It's a farm masquerading as a small United Nations. An array of flags pays tribute to the countries that fund the organization's work: creating better crops for the developing world's poor farmers.

Further ahead is a line of white signs, each standing in front of a small square plot where hairy heads of wheat sway in the breeze. This is agriculture's Walk of Fame; on those signs are the names of wheat varieties that emerged from CIMMYT's breeding grounds four decades ago: Sonora, Yaqui, Kauz, Sujata, Sonalika, and others. These varieties, which resist disease and produce unprecedented yields, conquered Asia, displacing traditional wheat varieties and older methods of farming. The stars of the Green Revolution, the new varieties unleashed a phenomenal rise in grain production that allowed China and India to feed themselves. Indeed, the impact of the new grains was so great that they earned Norman Borlaug, the original director of CIMMYT's wheat program, the Nobel Peace Prize in 1970. . . .

Reproduction of Staple Crops

The annual requirement for fresh seed is in part a consequence of corn's biological compulsion to mate freely and indiscriminately. Wheat, like rice, practices the safe sex of self-sex. Each flower pollinates itself, producing daughter plants that are nearly exact copies of their parents—at least that's the case with purebred wheat varieties such as those released by CIMMYT. As a result, farmers can use part of each year's harvest for seed, and varieties can easily be shared—passed from field to field, from one farmer to the next.

Corn, on the other hand, is the most promiscuous of plants. Its tassels—the male genitalia—dispense millions of pollen grains into the wind, randomly fertilizing nearby corn ears, the female genitalia. A plant's offspring, therefore, can vary enormously, depending on which pollen wandered into the neighborhood. So no matter how carefully CIMMYT's breeders construct improved varieties of corn, the genetic identity of those lines breaks down quickly when they are released into the genetic melting pot of farmers' fields. The new traits—higher yield, ability to withstand drought, resistance to disease—tend to dissipate and even disappear.

The variability problem is even greater with the hybrid varieties seed companies favor. For corn and even for self-pollinating plants, a hybrid's offspring are nothing like the original.

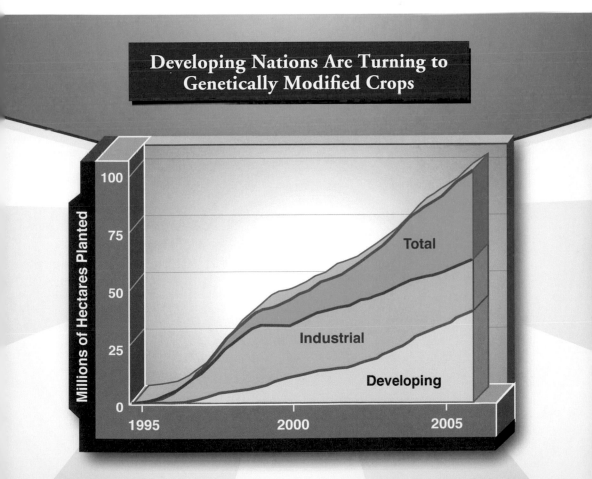

Developing Nations Are Turning to Genetically Modified Crops

Taken from: Terri Raney and Pirabhu Pingali, "Sowing a Gene Revolution," *Scientific American*, September 2007, p. 106.

Can Corn Be Cloned?

If only corn could reproduce by skipping pollination altogether and cloning itself. The idea is not as far-fetched as one might think. A few plants do this naturally, creating seeds without sex in a process called apomixis. Dandelions reproduce through apomixis; so do about 400 other plant species, including at least one wild relative of corn. So why not corn? If someone could flip a switch and make corn apomictic,

The most important genetically modified food in the developing world is rice.

CIMMYT might finally be able to make highly productive hardy strains poor farmers could share with their neighbors and replant from their own harvest year after year.

Richard Jefferson, founder of the Center for the Application of Molecular Biology to International Agriculture in Canberra, Australia, says that the implications of apomixis go well beyond corn. The potential of self-cloning plants, he says, is so profound and subversive that plant breeders, generally a cautious and understated lot, "would never admit to dreaming about it unless you got them drunk first."

In addition to bringing hybrid and other superior varieties of corn within reach of even the poorest farmer, apomixis would allow the widespread use of high yield hybrid rice, plants whose seeds currently are expensive and difficult to produce in large quantities. And apomixis could help eliminate diseases from cassava, an African staple crop that is grown by replanting pieces of tubers from parent plants, some of which carry disease.

FAST FACT

According to Collegians for a Constructive Tomorrow, U.S. farmers growing genetically modified crops increased their crop yields by 4 billion pounds.

The Apomixis of Corn

After more than a decade of work, researchers at CIMMYT and a handful of other laboratories around the world are finally homing in on apomixis. With the help of new genomic information and tools, they're tweaking the genes that control plant reproduction, hoping to duplicate the self-cloning process in corn and other important crops. If they succeed—and they seem confident that eventually, perhaps in another decade, they will—apomixis will open the door to a "revolution in world food production," says Wayne Hanna, a geneticist with the U.S. Department of Agriculture in Tifton, GA.

That may seem like a technology goal few could argue with. Yet there's uncertainty about whether apomixis ever will be allowed into farmers' fields. Two opposing forces could find themselves unlikely allies in an effort to block it: political opposition to genetic engineering and the financial considerations of agricultural companies that are among the primary sponsors of apomixis research. . . .

The Search for Apomixis Genes

In 1999 CIMMYT signed an agreement with a French seed company, Limagrain; a division of Swiss pharmaceutical giant Novartis that has since become Syngenta; and the world's largest seed company, Pioneer Hi-Bred. The agreement gave the center funding and access to private corn-genome databases. "The new tools have become so powerful," says [scientist Daniel] Grimanelli. "You can clone genes, modify genes, express genes." He and [Olivier] Leblanc [Grimanelli's colleague] embarked on a search for apomixis genes, sifting through the sections of DNA that were present in the apomictic form of gamma grass but not in the sexual version. They tracked those genes to a large block of DNA, about one-third of a chromosome, that is always present in the apomictic form of gamma grass. To find the specific genes in this huge field of DNA, the researchers are throwing transposons—small bits of DNA that insert themselves randomly into chromosomes—at that block of DNA. They're hoping that the transposons will insert themselves into genes that are important for apomixis, disrupting the process. When that occurs, the researchers should be able to locate the transposon and with it, the crucial gene— which they could then insert into corn. But the CIMMYT researchers are not alone in their search for the genetic keys to apomixis. A horde of other researchers, some of them sponsored by small biotech startups, have joined the hunt. Competing projects have sprouted in Germany, Switzerland, Australia, the United Kingdom, France, Mexico, California, Texas, and Utah. Most of the newcomers are not hoping to transfer apomixis genes from one species to another— from gamma grass to corn, for instance. Instead, they're tinkering with the timing of plants' own genes to trick them into reproducing without fertilization. The researchers are working out the details of this "synthetic" apomixis through experiments with their favorite "lab rat," a small mustard plant called *Arabidopsis thaliana*. The CIMMYT researchers, whose effort also is going to rely heavily on genomics data from better-known plants such as *Arabidopsis*, say the leap from *Arabidopsis* to corn is likely to be more difficult than many researchers expect. But still, they say, it will happen. The "incredible dynamism of so many people working on this," says Grimanelli, will not be denied. . . .

The Future of Apomictic Self-Cloning Corn

Even before the first apomictic self-cloning corn seeds are ready to be sown, the prospect looms that political debates and corporate interests will poison the ground. And that would be a blight not only on the future of poor farmers, but also on the reputation of agricultural biotechnology—a field already dogged by accusations that its science has not done enough for the human good.

Producing biotech crops that feed the poor and improve the lives of farmers in the developing world would convincingly refute such accusations. David Hoisington, director of CIMMYT's biotechnology program, believes that such crops are on their way. CIMMYT's first genetically engineered corn, a nonapomictic variety that repels the stem borer worm, is ready for field tests. In another decade or so, plots of apomictic corn could mark a new entry in the CIMMYT Walk of Fame. "The technology is such a powerful tool for solving problems," says Hoisington, "that it has to be accepted."

EVALUATING THE AUTHOR'S ARGUMENTS:

In the viewpoint you just read, the author claims that if corn could be cloned, then CIMMYT may be able to make strains that are highly productive and effective so that poor farmers could finally have enough crop to share with neighbors and to replant each year. Summarize the author's arguments for genetic engineering, and state whether you agree that the potential to stop world hunger is possible with genetically altered corn.

Viewpoint
4

Genetically Modified Food Can Decrease the World's Food Supply

David Kennell

"There is a good chance GM agriculture will lead to catastrophic famine in the world by greatly decreasing the gene pool of plants."

In the following viewpoint David Kennell argues that genetically modified crops can wreak havoc on the world's food supply. He explains that genetically modified crops eliminate plant diversity by dominating and wiping out non–genetically modified crops. These "super" seeds are stronger than non-engineered seeds and replace the traits of the original plants, thus reducing the bio-diversity of plant varieties. But biodiversity is important because it protects crops from becoming extinct, he explains. Should one crop of potato fail, another crop from a dif-ferent seed will thrive, ensuring the survival of at least some potatoes. But if all potatoes are from the same strain of seed, potatoes could be wiped out in the event of a blight, famine, or other crop disaster. In this way, Kennell warns, genetically modified crops increase the risk of food shortages. The best

David Kennell, "Genetically Engineered Plant Crops: Potential for Disaster," *Synthesis/Regeneration,* vol. 35, Fall 2004, p. 11. Reproduced by permission.

way to prevent these disasters, he says, is to ensure that the biodiversity of plant species remains protected. The author concludes that more species result in a more plentiful food supply.

Kennell is professor emeritus at the Department of Molecular Microbiology at Washington University School of Medicine.

AS YOU READ, CONSIDER THE FOLLOWING QUESTIONS:
1. Name at least three crop disasters that the author says have contributed to famines.
2. What is "homogenization," and why is it bad for crops, according to Kennell?
3. Why would a reduction in the gene pool of plants result in an increase in world hunger, according to the author?

Genetic Engineered Plant Crops-Potential for Disaster

Transgenic crops will greatly accelerate the decline of biodiversity in the plant world. Reason: Seed corporations demand farmers buy seed from them each year—replacing the millennial practice of farmers selecting seeds best suited for their specific environments. By coercing governments of developing countries to plant genetically-modified (GM) crops, much of the native crops are replaced by a monoculture of the GM crop for export to meet the country's debt. The country then has to import food to replace their native crops.

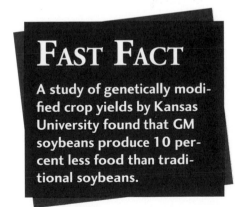

FAST FACT

A study of genetically modified crop yields by Kansas University found that GM soybeans produce 10 percent less food than traditional soybeans.

Once GM plants are introduced, farmers may be unable to grow non-GM crops. The famous Percy Schmeiser case in Saskatchewan, Canada has dramatized what is occurring on farms all over the world and relates to the broader issue of patents on life. The unintended spread of glyphosate-resistant pollen from Round-up Ready (RR) canola plants (possibly by wind, birds, trucks, etc.) contaminated Schmeiser's non-GM canola fields. Even though they agreed that he never planted or wanted Monsanto's GM seeds, two lower Courts ruled that he had to pay patent fees to Monsanto. The case was accepted by the Canadian Supreme Court which ruled on May 21, 2004 by a close five to four margin that the patent rights did apply. They applied to the engineered genes rather than to the plants. This decision was disappointing to the thousands of Schmeiser supporters around the world.

However, the Court also ruled that a Corporation would have to prove that a farmer profited from the unintended use of a bioengineered crop in his field. Since it was agreed that Schmeiser made no additional profit from the contaminating RR canola, he was not required to pay Monsanto for profits, penalties, court costs, or the technology use fee ($15/acre). Unfortunately, the superior seeds he had selected during 50 years of plantings had been lost by contamination. More recently, on March 19, 2008 in an out-of-court settlement, Monsanto agreed to pay all costs to clean-up the RR canola that contaminated his fields.

However, the ecological damage was done. The University of Manitoba found that 32 of the 33 commercially available seed lots of native canola have been contaminated with RR seeds. The canola of the Great Plains is rapidly becoming a monoculture variety which carries the potential for disaster. The RR plants have even invaded other crop species—in such case becoming like a "super-weed". This experience was not unique and is happening to agricultural crops all over the world.

Why is biodiversity important? The great Russian botanist Nikolai Vavilov, traveled the world collecting and categorizing plants and seeds. He proposed that there are 8 centers of origin of the major species of food plants, all in Third World countries, e.g., corn-Mexico; rice-India; Andes mountains-potatoes, tomatoes; China-soybeans. There have been dozens of major crop disasters in our world in the last 150 years following the great potato blight famine in Ireland in the 1840s. A few examples:

- 1870s: coffee rust in Ceylon, India, East Asia, Africa (reason England is a nation of tea drinkers).
- 1890s: cotton epidemic.
- 1904: 1916, 1954, stem rust in US wheat (75% of wheat lost in 1954).
- 1940s: brown spot disease of Indian rice (Bengal famine).

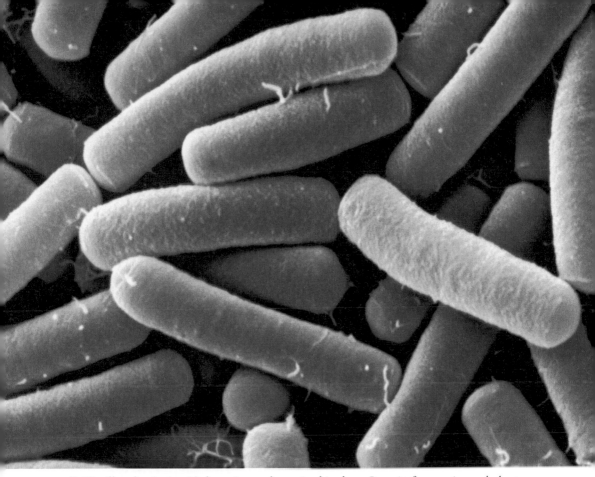

Bt (Bacillus thuringiensis) *bacteria are shown in this photo. Bt toxin from engineered plants is more stable than the natural toxins of* B.thuringiensis.

- 1940s and again in 1950s: 80% of US oat crop.
- 1940s: USSR wheat crop; led to huge Russian grain deal.
- 1970s: corn blight (*Bipolaris*) in US destroyed 15% of corn crop.
- 1980: French grapes; aphid powdery mildew (France turned to the US for resistant germplasm).
- 1990s: Russet Burbank potato is high in mass/water (reason is used for McDonalds fries) (*Phytophthora infestans* potato blight) spread over the world.

Each time resistance was needed. Each time it was most likely found in centers of origin in landraces that had escaped "homogenization."

Vavilov observed: These centers are also centers of greatest diversity of varieties and also a rich source of genetic alleles for resistance to specific crop diseases, having evolved varieties during millions of years through many different environments and diseases.

For example, a worthless-looking primordial wheat plant from Turkey is primitive progenitor in all breeding programs of U.S. wheat. By 1984, 58% of U.S. wheat used original germplasm—it was only 7% in 1969.

GM plants disrupt the normal ecology selected in millions of years of evolution with some unknown and some known consequences. The incorporated foreign resistance genes provide only short-term advantage. Nature selects for strains resistant to them, e.g., resistance to round-up is increasing: goosegrass in Malaysia, Italian ryegrass, Australian ryegrass, Horseweed in the US. Now, over 500 species are resistant to pesticides and over 100 weed species are resistant to herbicides. Pesticide use is up more than 1000 fold on corn since 1945 but corn crop losses increased from 3.5% to 12% in the same period of time.

Concurrently, many beneficial insects and microorganisms are killed by the pesticides, and by the added "inerts" that account for most of bulk (they are not identified even though many are toxic). Bt toxin from engineered plants is much more stable than the natural toxin from *B. thuringiensis.* It can remain potent for months in the soil. A teaspoon of soil contains millions of bacteria and fungi, as well as arthropods and earthworms. Soil is a living environment that is unique for each specific place on the planet after millions of years of evolution. It is estimated that one inch of topsoil took 500 years to evolve.

Solutions: Return to practice of crop rotations. In 1945 corn was grown in rotation with soybeans, wheat and other crops. Corn on corn (increased with GM-agriculture) promotes survival of disease vectors and weeds specific for corn. Also, there is increased water runoff and soil erosion. Data for cases where yields have been reduced from GM-crops compared to non-GM crops are accumulating. Also, rotation provides more home-grown food and self-sufficiency.

The United Nations World Food Program concluded that there is 1.5 times the food needed to feed all people. Hunger is a problem of food distribution and of returning land to native farming. GM-crops have *nothing* to do with solving hunger; in fact, there is a good chance GM agriculture will lead to catastrophic famine in the world by greatly decreasing the gene pool of plants and by major disruption of the ecology of life that has evolved over millions of years. Foreign genes inserted at random sites automatically cause two or more unknown mutations in a host genome, creating unknown phenotypes.

No one knows the consequences of hundreds of man-made life forms being spread across our planet! It is a completely uncontrolled experiment that has no boundaries.

The only purpose of the promotion of GM plants is to control the world's food supply and thus guarantee continuing and increasing profits for the multinational agrichemical corporations.

EVALUATING THE AUTHORS' ARGUMENTS:

In this viewpoint the author explains that genetically modified food crops disrupt the natural evolution of plant species, which in turn hurts the world's food supply. The author of the preceding viewpoint, Daniel Charles, insists that genetically modified crops increase the world's food supply by making farmland more productive. After reading both viewpoints, with which author's perspective do you agree? Identify what piece of evidence or point of reasoning convinced you.

Genetically Modified Crops Help Third World Nations

John Semmens

"It is not so easy for people living in constant danger of malnutrition to wait for more evidence that genetically modified foods are perfectly safe."

In the following viewpoint John Semmens argues that genetically modified food can benefit third world nations. The author explains that planting genetically modified crops in these countries can increase the food supply and open more farming opportunities. Semmens also claims that genetically engineered food can provide third world nations with food that is fortified with vitamins and nutrients. This is important, as people in these countries often lack adequate amounts of vitamins and nutrients. More nutritious food can reduce the occurrence of diseases common in malnourished people, such as blindness. Whether genetically modified food provides farming opportunities for starving people or whether it provides nutritional supplements to make people healthier, Semmens concludes that genetic engineering helps people in third world nations.

John Semmens, "Freedom Is the Environment's Best Friend," *Freeman*, vol. 57, April 2007, pp. 10–12.
Copyright © 2007 Foundation for Economic Education, Incorporated. www.fee.org. All rights reserved. Reproduced by permission.

Semmens is a transportation policy analyst at the Laissez Faire Institute in Arizona.

AS YOU READ, CONSIDER THE FOLLOWING QUESTIONS:
1. Why is it easier for rich people to be skeptical about genetically modified foods than poor people, according to the author?
2. What does the author say is the main difference between current genetic engineering techniques and those methods of previous years?
3. How has technology made farming more efficient, according to the author?

Every April 22 celebrations of Earth Day take place around the world. This can serve as a reminder to reflect on the status of our planet. Some believe the earth is in great peril and that stringent measures to restrain economic development and technology are necessary to avoid a horrible fate. . . .

Genetically Engineered Crops Can Feed Third World Nations

A . . . key concept of environmental alarmists is the so-called "precautionary principle." The idea here is that anything that entails any amount of risk is to be shunned or prevented from happening. According to this way of thinking, only when it is proven beyond a reasonable doubt to be safe should such a product or activity be permitted.

An example of the precautionary principle in action is the environmental alarmists' protest against genetically modified foods. Scientists can now use gene-splicing to engineer more favorable traits into food. "Golden rice" is one of the products developed by this technique. This genetically modified rice incorporates more vitamin A into the plant. The benefit of this is that it enables people whose diets are over-dependent on rice (as is the case in many Third World countries) to obtain sufficient amounts of this vitamin to ward off blindness. This is not to say that everyone who eats plain rice will go blind. However, a distressingly large portion of the children in Third World countries do go blind from insufficient quantities of vitamin A in their diets.

Despite the beneficial attributes of golden rice, it is still a genetically modified "Frankenfood" to many environmental alarmists. The gene-splicing necessary to create golden rice is unnatural. It could have unforeseen consequences. It would be better, argue advocates of the precautionary principle, to wait until it can be proven to be totally safe before its widespread introduction into the food supply.

FAST FACT

According to the International Service of Agri-Biotech Applications, 90 percent of farmers growing genetically modified crops in 2007 were resource-poor farmers from twelve developing countries.

It is easy for the affluent and well fed, who can supplement abundant food supplies with vitamins, minerals, and herbal nutrients, to be cautious about new, untried, genetically modified foods. No one is saying these people must eat these innovations. But it is not so easy for people living in constant danger of malnutrition to wait for more evidence that genetically modified foods are perfectly safe.

Further, the notion that genetically modified foods are a recent innovation ignores the thousands of years of human genetic "tampering" with nature that has produced many agricultural products we take for granted. There was never a time when the type of cows that produce our milk ran free and wild. Modern milk cows are the outcome of thousands of years of selective breeding that has modified the genetic make up of these creatures.

Genetic Modifications Are Not a New Concept

A similar story can be told about the corn-on-the-cob we chow down on at picnics. American Indians nurtured this hybrid through cross-fertilization of carefully selected weeds. Or how about that pet Chihuahua at the end of your leash? Ever see a pack of them run down prey on one of those nature shows?

The fact is, people have been genetically modifying other living creatures for thousands of years. It's just that earlier methods were less predictable and more time-consuming than modern gene-splicing methods. We are doing what we have always done—changing the world to make it more to our liking.

If the precautionary-principle zealots had walked among our cave-dwelling ancestors, they probably would have tried to prevent the use of fire. It's dangerous and polluting. It has killed far more people than nuclear energy—a modern substitute in many uses. Yet, even today, environmental alarmists oppose replacing coal-fired electricity with nuclear-generated electricity.

The precautionary principle takes a healthy skepticism about the new and untried (after all, most new ideas are a flop; only a minority ultimately succeed) and turns it into a stultifying phobia. Progress requires that we take calculated risks in the effort to make things better. The track record of science and technology in this regard should be a source of confidence. The human mind is an amazing tool. It ought not to be tied down by irrational fears. . . .

Genetically Modified Crops Are Profitable

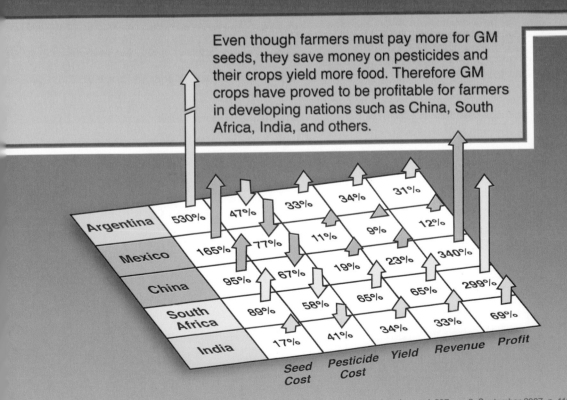

Even though farmers must pay more for GM seeds, they save money on pesticides and their crops yield more food. Therefore GM crops have proved to be profitable for farmers in developing nations such as China, South Africa, India, and others.

	Seed Cost	Pesticide Cost	Yield	Revenue	Profit
Argentina	530%	47%	33%	34%	31%
Mexico	165%	77%	11%	9%	12%
China	95%	67%	19%	23%	340%
South Africa	89%	58%	65%	65%	299%
India	17%	41%	34%	33%	69%

Taken from: Terri Raney and Pirabhu Pingali, "Sowing a Gene Revolution," *Scientific American*, vol. 297, no. 3, September 2007, p. 110.

Proponents of GM foods say that anti-GM activists do not consider that people living on the edge of subsistence cannot afford to conserve their environment.

Genetically Engineered Foods Increase Food Supplies

The environmental alarmists have it backwards. If anything imperils the earth it is ignorant obstruction of science and progress. People living on the edge of subsistence cannot afford to conserve the environment. Their energies must go into surviving. People who are prosperous can afford to think about conserving the environment. So to the extent that the measures demanded by environmental alarmists retard progress, they also endanger the environment.

That technology provides the best option for serving human wants and conserving the environment should be evident in the progress made in environmental improvement in the United States. Virtually every measure shows that pollution is headed downward and that nature is making a comeback.

A few years ago I visited the historical site of "the shot heard round the world"—Lexington, Concord, and Battle Road in Massachusetts. The area is lush with trees and greenery. Park Rangers explain that in 1775 the area was void of this greenery. The trees were chopped down to make way for farming. In those days farming was so much less efficient than today that 80 percent of the population had to engage in it to provide enough food to feed the nation. Vast swaths of countryside had to be leveled for the low-yielding crops of that era.

Technology has changed all that. Pesticides and genetically modified crops have allowed more of the fruits and vegetables to escape being eaten by insects. Better transportation has enabled more food to get to market before spoiling. Refrigeration has allowed food to stay edible longer. As a result, the portion of the workforce needed for agriculture has dropped to 2 percent. Massachusetts farmland has been allowed to revert to forest.

This is the model for saving the rest of the planet: let freedom to think and trade make use of the genius of humanity for a better world.

EVALUATING THE AUTHOR'S ARGUMENTS:

In this viewpoint the author expresses frustration with the "precautionary principle," which states that an action should not be taken without 100 percent certainty that it will do no harm. Explain why he rejects the precautionary principle as it pertains to genetically modified foods, and state which you think hurts hungry people more—banning or eating genetically modified food.

Genetically Modified Crops Hurt Third World Nations

Bob Phelps, Judy Carman, and Mae-Wan Ho

"[Genetically modified crops] will destroy the diversity, the local knowledge and the sustainable agricultural systems that our farmers have developed for millennia."

In the following viewpoint Bob Phelps, Judy Carman, and Mae-Wan Ho argue that genetically modified crops intended to alleviate hunger will actually hurt hungry people living in third world nations. They explain that many of these communities are a collection of agricultural societies that have existed for thousands of years and rely on sustainable agricultural practices to live. But when genetically modified crops are introduced into their area, traditional farming land is displaced, food production of other essential crops declines, widespread flooding and forest clearing destroys land, and the introduction of toxic weed killers threatens plant biodiversity. Therefore, the authors urge third world nations to embrace sustainable farming practices to preserve the environment and protect their ability to grow crops. The authors conclude that

Bob Phelps, Judy Carman, and Mae-Wan Ho, "Genetically Engineered Crops Can't 'Feed the World,'" *Issues*, vol. 69, December 2004, pp. 18–20. Reproduced by permission.

genetically modified crops threaten crop yields and reduce the amount of food for third world people, and as such should be rejected.

Phelps is director of the Australian GeneEthics Network, which debates the environmental, social, and ethical impacts of gene technology. Ho is a cofounder and director at the Institute of Science in Society, a nonprofit organization that promotes public understanding of critical science issues.

AS YOU READ, CONSIDER THE FOLLOWING QUESTIONS:
1. Who is Wangari Maathi and why does she warn Africans to reject GM crops, according to the authors?
2. According to the authors, how have genetically modified crops impacted Argentina's agricultural society and environment?
3. Why are GM crops a poor choice in the face of impending oil shortages and climate change, according to the authors?

Genetically modified (GM) crops cannot solve world hunger. Those currently grown commercially—soy, corn, canola and cotton—are usually less productive than conventional crops. For example, GM soy productivity in the USA is 5–10% lower. GM soy also requires more chemicals overall. GM crops that are proposed for future production of drugs and industrial materials, such as plastics, would further reduce food production.

Genetically Modified Foods Do Not Adequately Address Hunger

At least, 700 million people are starving or malnourished globally and thousands die of starvation daily as food is unfairly distributed, unavailable or unaffordable. World food production is one-and-a-half times enough to feed everyone adequately. About three-quarters of the regions where people starve also export commodities such as tea, coffee, sugar, cotton and animal fodder to privileged countries.

Crop failures or other natural disasters, civil conflicts and wars, markets distorted by farm subsidies in rich countries, and foreign debt repayments all deny people the adequate, balanced diets needed for good health. These social and structural reasons for hunger can only be solved with political will, not gene technology.

For example, GM "golden rice" is proposed as a possible way to prevent blindness among children in poorer countries who suffer from vitamin A deficiency. This affronts the rights of malnourished people to have a balanced diet—including green leafy vegetables, fruit, meat, fish, eggs or milk products—which naturally contain enough Vitamin A for good health. Anyway, the small amounts of Vitamin A genetically engineered into golden rice could not be assimilated without a balanced diet. Vitamin A rice is therefore irrelevant to feeding people or preventing disease, but this idea is widely promoted as a reason that Australia should accept GM crops and foods.

Third World Nations Should Be Wary of Genetically Engineered Foods

Twenty-four African countries denounced public relations campaigns that promote GM foods in a statement to the United Nations in 1999. They said:

> . . . the image of the poor and hungry is being used by giant multinational corporations to push a technology that is neither safe, environmentally friendly, nor economically beneficial to us. We do not believe that such companies or gene technologies will help our farmers to produce the food that is needed in the 21st century. On the contrary, we think it will destroy the diversity, the local knowledge and the sustainable agricultural systems that our farmers have developed for millennia and that it will thus undermine our capacity to feed ourselves.

To promote their products, GM companies and the U.S. government's foreign aid program (USAID) developed Kenya as a GM industry bridgehead in Africa, prompting Kenyan Nobel Peace Prize winner Wangari Maathai to warn:

> Biotechnology and patenting of life forms is now the new frontier for conquest, and Africa ought to be wary because a history of colonialism and exploitation is repeating itself.

The World Food Program also misuses food aid to push GM crops into African countries. For instance, starving people in Zimbabwe and Zambia were denied food when the US government refused to process corn prior to sending it there. The gene contamination of native corn varieties experienced in Mexico had warned African governments that raw grains delivered as food aid might be planted, so that pollen and seed may threaten local cropping systems and export markets.

The Group of 77 Third World Nations and China—led by Ethiopia—strongly supports the Biosafety Protocol, which aims to make the international transfer of GM organisms safer. In contrast, the USA, Canada, Argentina and Australia—all major grain exporting nations—will not join the Protocol.

FAST FACT

Although Argentina is the world's second largest producer of GM crops, according to a Friends of the Earth report, millions of Argentineans are facing hunger and malnutrition.

Genetically Modified Crops Have High Social and Environmental Costs

Argentina's GM soybean monocultures, which are resistant to Roundup herbicide, show the terrible social and environmental costs of GM crops. Impacts in Argentina include:

- 500 rural villages have been abandoned or destroyed;
- 160,000 rural people—one-third of the rural populace—have been dispossessed of their land and livelihoods and are now living in urban shanties;
- there have been sharp declines in other means of food production that gave local people balanced diets;
- there has been widespread flooding from soil compaction in Roundup-based no-till farming systems;
- accelerated forest clearing has contributed to flooding and biodiversity loss; and
- Roundup-tolerant superweeds and volunteer soy plants are managed with toxic weedkillers.

Critics say that in Zambia people were denied food when the U.S. government refused to process food to be free of gene contamination before shipping it there.

The GM industry plans a huge GM soybean invasion of South America. Agrochemical giant Syngenta's advertisement—"Soybean knows no frontiers"—labels a map of Argentina, Brazil, Paraguay and Bolivia as the "United Republic of Soy". Syngenta's chemical controls soybean rust, which is spreading with GM Roundup-tolerant soy. . . .

Sustainable Farming Is a Better Solution

Industrial agriculture depends heavily on oil and water, both of which are rapidly running out, and GM crops will intensify that dependence. It is very energy-intensive, and is getting increasingly unproductive as the soil is depleted, causing erosion and flash floods. The only way to feed the world is sustainable agriculture, which will also serve to soften the worst excesses of climate change.

An excellent recent example of successful sustainable farm practices is in Ethiopia, traditionally the "famine capital" of the world. In 1995, Ethiopia's Environment Protection Authority and the Institute of Sustainable Development introduced traditional Indian pit composting together with simple water and soil conservation techniques into the northern state of Tigray. Crop yields have more than doubled, outperforming chemical fertilisers in most cases and transforming degraded land into productive greenery. The Ethiopian government has now adopted organic agriculture as a major strategy for food security, delivering good quality, nutritious food, free from agrochemicals and a clean environment, which are crucial for delivering good health.

This is what every country in the world should be doing, rich or poor. The small organic family farm, also typical in Africa, is the best option for soybean farming as it creates rural work and a good sustainable life by effectively harnessing minimum resources. In contrast, research found the GM herbicide-based no-tillage option would increase landlessness and transfer wealth to elites.

Genetically Modified Foods Cannot Feed the World

GM is not the robust global answer to hunger that industry would have us believe. GM crops are:

- just 1.37% of global agriculture (68 million hectares of GM in 18 countries; all farms are 5 million hectares in 218 countries);
- 97.5% grown in only five countries—the USA (62.4%), Argentina (20.2%), Canada (6.4%), Brazil (4.4%) and China (4.1%). Australia's GM cotton is 0.15% of the total;
- 92%-owned by Monsanto, the main beneficiary;
- engineered with just two traits—herbicide tolerance (so farmers can spray more) and insect toxin (that kills some caterpillars); and
- not a growth industry since 1999 (except for Roundup-tolerant soy) as the acreages of GM corn, cotton and canola have stopped expanding.

The global GM food and cropping industry's claims of being able to "feed the world" are false and discredited. The relentless, unscrupulous and unethical quest for monopoly control of the global food supply, especially through patents on life promoted by the US government, has failed. All governments should review their uncritical commitment to gene technology, and adopt ethical solutions to hunger.

EVALUATING THE AUTHORS' ARGUMENTS:

In this viewpoint Phelps and Ho blame genetically modified crops for damaging, and in some cases destroying, third world agricultural communities. What pieces of evidence did the authors provide to support their claim? Did they convince you of their argument? Explain why or why not.

Genetically Modified Seeds Threaten Farmers

"Even farmers who obtain GE seed intentionally and legally have to sign an agreement not to save it [for the following farming season]."

Katherine Whitworth

In the following viewpoint Katherine Whitworth argues that genetically modified seeds threaten independent farmers' way of life. For centuries, farmers have saved money by harvesting the seeds from one crop cycle and planting them the following season. But genetically modified seeds are often engineered to be sterile and thus are unable to be used from one planting cycle to the next. This means that farmers are forced to buy new seeds each growing season, which they can rarely afford. For this reason, Whitworth concludes that genetically modified seeds make farmers beholden to large corporations who own the patents for genetically modified seeds.

Whitworth has written several articles for the *Arkansas Times*.

Katherine Whitworth, "Frankenfood," *Arkansas Times*, vol. 33, March 8, 2007, p. 16. Reproduced by permission.

AS YOU READ, CONSIDER THE FOLLOWING QUESTIONS:
  1. According to the author, what did the development of geneti-
     cally modified plants pave the way for?
  2. In what case might a farmer be sued by a GM seed company,
     according to the authors?
  3. In what way might a GM seed "commit suicide," according to
     Whitworth?

The Arkansas Plant Board voted last week to ban the planting of the second variety of rice found in Arkansas to contain traces of a genetically engineered variety of rice. With no disrespect to the farmers who protested the ruling and are now scrambling to make up for the lost seed, I'd like to give the Plant Board a round of applause.

The Board's argument is that many foreign countries are so skeptical about the safety of genetically engineered (GE) foods that they will either refuse to import them or will accept them only at drastically reduced prices. Export accounts for about half of all U.S. rice sales, so from an economic standpoint, it makes sense to ban production of something that will likely go unsold. But the reasons for rejecting GE foods go far beyond simple economics.

Genetically Modified Plants Are Dangerous

Two basic types of genetic modification are important here: plants that have been bred to be herbicide-resistant, allowing for (ahem, requiring) blanket application of companion weed killers; and plants that self-produce insect-killing bacteria, the seeds of which are themselves classified as insecticide. The development of these new genetic technologies in turn helped pave the way for the widespread patenting of genes.

So what's the hubbub? Depends on what you're afraid of. Maybe you're an environmentalist and you reason that consistent spraying of one chemical on one type of plant will inevitably lead to the evolution of weeds and pests that are resistant to that chemical, which will in turn necessitate even more spraying, and more resistance, causing a vicious cycle.

Or maybe you want to avoid stuff that may be harmful to you. One method of forcing modified genes into the DNA of a given

Out-of-Control Crops

Since 1996 dozens of instances of GM contamination, illegal plantings, and negative agricultural side effects have occurred throughout the world. Even though it would not be the farmer's fault if a GM seed contaminated their crop, they could be sued by the GM seed's patent holder for illegal use of the seed.

Country	Count	Country	Count
Argentina	2	Japan	9
Australia	9	Kuwait	1
Austria	5	Luxembourg	1
Belgium	1	Malta	1
Bolivia	2	Mexico	8
Brazil	7	Netherlands	6
Bulgaria	2	New Zealand	0
Canada	10	Nicaragua	2
Chile	1	Norway	1
China	4	Peru	2
Colombia	1	Philippines	3
Croatia	2	Poland	2
Cyprus	3	Romania	6
Czech Republic	1	Russia	1
Denmark	3	Serbia	1
Egypt	1	Sierra Leone	1
Equador	1	Slovenia	1
Europe-wide	1	South Africa	1
Finland	3	South Korea	2
France	12	Spain	3
Germany	15	Sweden	4
Ghana	1	Switzerland	2
Greece	4	Taiwan	1
Guatemala	1	Thailand	3
Hungary	1	UAE	1
India	4	UK	14
Ireland	4	USA	24

Taken from: GeneWatch UK/Greenpeace International.

Soy farmer Homan McFarling is fighting Monsanto in court over the ancient agricultural practice of saving seeds from a previous harvest. Monsanto wants farmers to pay for what once was free.

plant involves invading the target plant's cells with bacteria like E. coli. Ick. Also, antibiotic-resistant "marker genes"—which could lead to the evolution of antibiotic-resistant infections—are often included in these modified sequences purely for testing the success of the construction. The USDA [United States Department of Agriculture] and FDA [Food and Drug Administration] insist that GE foods are completely safe to eat, despite having done little or no testing to support their claims.

Generally Modified Seeds Hurt Farmers' Livelihood

We also don't know much about how GE plants may mutate over time. Engineering a gene isn't quite the same as designing, say, a new car. Living organisms mutate and cross-pollinate and reproduce, and there's simply no telling what these "frankenfoods" (is a tomato bred with pig DNA still considered vegetarian, or Kosher, for that matter?) will become several generations down the line.

Thanks to those patents, we may never get to find out. For thousands of years, one way many farmers have been able to afford to continue farming is by saving seed from each crop to plant the following year. This is also how, sometimes over generations, farmers have developed seed that is suited specifically to the conditions in which it is grown. Now suppose you're a small family farmer and some patented GE seed blows off a truck, or is carried by the wind from a neighboring farm, and your conventional crop becomes "contaminated" with it.

Because the patent applies to the GE gene, and the gene travels from one generation to the next, all of your subsequent crops now belong to the holder of the patent, which is almost certainly one of only four U.S. seed companies. You will be sued. Even though you did nothing intentionally wrong, the courts (based on rulings so far) will side with big business. Your seed stores will be destroyed. You will go bankrupt. Or you'll settle, at a significant financial loss. The kicker: even farmers who obtain GE seed intentionally and legally have to sign an agreement not to save it.

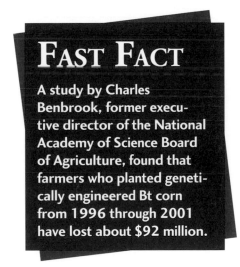

FAST FACT

A study by Charles Benbrook, former executive director of the National Academy of Science Board of Agriculture, found that farmers who planted genetically engineered Bt corn from 1996 through 2001 have lost about $92 million.

Genetically Engineered Seeds Benefit Big Business

Talk about paranoid. Several years ago, a company called Delta & Pine Land Co. (whose soybean operations are in Harrisburg, Ark.), developed a nifty little thing called the "Terminator gene." This gene causes a plant to effectively commit suicide, by producing sterile seed. They might not release it commercially, but we've already established that seed has a way of getting around on its own. This is an obvious attempt on the part of the seed companies to ensure that their products—seeds and chemicals, now largely interdependent—continue to be bought; the USDA says as much on its web site. You don't have to be a conspiracy theorist to imagine the potential implications.

EVALUATING THE AUTHOR'S ARGUMENTS:

In this viewpoint Katherine Whitworth uses persuasive reasoning to support her argument that genetically modified seeds hurt farmers. She does not, however, use any quotations to support her ideas. If you were to rewrite this article and insert quotations, what authorities might you quote from? Where would you place these quotations to bolster the points Whitworth makes?

Genetically Modified Seeds Do Not Threaten Farmers

"Nearly three-quarters of the state's soybean farmers have been planting transgenic seeds for years."

Tony Smith

In the following viewpoint Tony Smith argues that genetically modified seeds do not hurt farmers' abilities to grow crops. Gene-altered crops have been successfully grown for years in the United States, Canada, and Argentina, and are now being planted by farmers in other countries around the world, the author claims. Smith explains that transgenic, or genetically altered, crops often produce higher yields than traditional crops as a result of built-in chemicals that repel weeds and insects. This decreases farmers' need to use expensive spray pesticides, saving them time and money. In addition, fewer weeds make genetically engineered crops easier to harvest. The author concludes that GM technology makes food production profitable for farmers, especially in third world nations.

Tony Smith has written several articles about soybeans for the *New York Times*.

Tony Smith, "Farmers Help Deliver Modified Crops to Brazil," *New York Times,* October 14, 2003. Copyright © 2003 by The New York Times Company. Reproduced by permission.

AS YOU READ, CONSIDER THE FOLLOWING QUESTIONS:
  1. How much has Brazil's soybean production increased in the last
     six years, according to the author?
  2. How many more bushels per acre have farmers in Santo Ângelo,
     Brazil, harvested as a result of using GM seeds, reports Smith?
  3. How much more does it cost to produce a metric ton of tra-
     ditional crops vs. genetically modified crops, according to the
     author?

Brazil's decision in late September [2003] to legalize the plant-ing of genetically modified soybeans may have infuriated environmentalists and some in the government, but it has caused much rejoicing and relief in the farming community here in Rio Grande do Sul, Brazil's southernmost state, where farmers have been planting transgenic soybeans illegally for years.

Among those celebrating is Rafael Moreno, who for the last four years has been planting and harvesting genetically engineered soybeans on his 1,000-acre farm. "Everybody around here was doing it and it made economic sense, so I did it, too," said Mr. Moreno, 30, a resident of this sleepy town close to the Argentine border.

Legalizing Genetically Engineered Seeds Is Beneficial to Farmers

Such realities and the fact that Brazil—already the world's No. 2 soybean producer, after the United States—is working hard to become an agricultural superpower are crucial factors behind President Luiz Inácio Lula da Silva's changed stance on the planting of genetically modified crops.

Before taking office in January, Mr. da Silva opposed such crops. But now that he heads the government, he has to weigh the growing importance of agribusiness, which accounted for a third of the country's gross domestic product and 40 percent of its exports last year.

Farmers here expect the president's decision, which legalized transgenic crops for this planting season, to pave the way for more permanent legislation that would put them on an equal footing with farmers in the United States, Argentina and Canada, where gene-altered crops have been planted for years.

Mr. da Silva's about-face will affect not only Brazilian farmers, but American exporters and consumers from Stockholm to Shanghai. "Now we'll be more competitive in everything—not just soy but melons, corn, oranges, cotton," Mr. Moreno said. "So far, we've only been catching up, thanks to our favorable climate and soil."

Genetically Modified Crops Are Profitable for Farmers

When Mr. Moreno started planting the seeds, originally smuggled from Argentina, most of his farm equipment was at least 15 years old—"more or less scrap metal," he said. But now, after just a few years, increasing returns from the farm have enabled him to replace all but one tractor.

The government's decision has also brought a palpable change in mood to a bustling tractor and farm machinery dealership in Santo Ângelo.

Genetically modified soybean seeds allow farmers to save on herbicide and fields of GM plants are free of weeds.

Just five years ago, local farmers' margins were shrinking, and Wilson Pippi, the owner of Pippi Máquinas, said he was finding it tough to drum up new business. But then more and more farmers began planting genetically modified soybeans smuggled from Argentina, and Mr. Pippi's sales took off.

"I've been selling Massey Ferguson [agricultural machinery] for 40 years, and I can't recall a more favorable outlook for agriculture round here," said Mr. Pippi, who also grows soybeans. Unwilling to put his other business at risk by breaking the law, Mr. Pippi had refrained from planting genetically modified soybeans, but now he says he will and predicts most Brazilian farmers will do the same.

> **FAST FACT**
>
> A 2006 IMRB International study showed Indian farmers who planted genetically engineered cotton seed saw a 118 percent increase in profit, a 25 percent reduction in pesticide costs, and a 64 percent increase in yield.

On a national scale, although only about 17 percent of the soy plants in Brazil's fields are transgenic, the country's soybean production has risen nearly 60 percent in the last six years, closing the gap on the United States, which is expecting a drought-diminished harvest in 2003. On Oct. 10 [2003], the United States said that Brazil was about to surpass it in soybean exports.

Santo Ângelo farmers say that by planting the genetically modified seeds their average yield has already risen from around 30 to nearly 50 bushels an acre. "Unlike farmers in America or Europe, Brazilian farmers get no subsidies, so this is important in helping us compete," Mr. Pippi said.

Genetically Modified Crops Are Easier to Harvest than Traditional Crops

Too much genetically modified soy, however, could pose a problem. Brazil's top export market for soybeans is the European Union, which has introduced stringent regulations on the origins of all genetically modified food because of concerns by consumers. Domestic consumers could also prove resistant.

The Genetically Modified World

Twenty-two countries, both industrial (blue) and developing (brown), grow genetically modified crops. The map below presents a selection of facts about the development and commercial production of transgenic (genetically altered) crops in developing nations; much more is under way.

China
- On the brink of approving Bt rice for commercial cultivation.
- Only developing country where farmers are cultivating transgenic crops (insect-resistant cotton) developed independently of the international private sector.

Iran
- Only country to approve Bt (insect-resistant) rice for commercial cultivation.

The Philippines
- Field trials of locally adapted Golden Rice to begin in late 2007.

Argentina
- Tremendous increase in soybean production credited to profitable transgenics.

Eastern Africa
- Maize streak virus is endemic.

India
- Indian researchers have developed transgenic eggplant, maize, pigeon pea, mustard, tomato, rice, okra, cabbage, and cauliflower. Initial small-scale field trials are under way.

Africa in General
- Staple crops with no transgenic varieties yet available: sorghum, chickpea, cassava, pearl millet, pigeon pea, and groundnut.

South Africa
- First developing country to plant a transgenic staple food (2001, Bt white maize).
- University researchers developed maize resistant to maize streak virus.
- Preliminary work is under way on developing maize tolerant of drought based on genes from plants indigenous to Africa.

Bangladesh, China, India Indonesia, the Philippines, South Africa, Vietnam
- Research institutes are working with Syngenta to develop locally adapted varieties of Golden Rice.

Taken from: Terri Raney and Pirabhu Pingali, "Sowing a Gene Revolution," *Scientific American*, September 2007, p. 106.

The stance in Europe appears to be softening considerably from three years ago, when genetically modified foods were described as Frankenfoods. But if Europeans continue to resist, "we will just have to look for other markets," said Amauri Miotto of Rio Grande's Fetag, a federation of farmers working small, family-owned properties. "There are plenty of poor, hungry people in the world who need cheaper food."

There is no reason Brazilian farmers cannot produce both conventional and genetically modified soybeans, said Carlo Lovatelli, president of the Brazilian Association of Vegetable Oil Industries, or ABIOVE, though he said they should be paid a premium for conventional crops because they cost $20 to $30 a metric ton more to produce.

Detailed labeling and testing required for export shipments will eat into the improved margins of those planting genetically modified soybeans. Farmers here, however, say those costs are marginal compared with the savings on herbicides and in time, because the fields of genetically modified soybeans are free of weeds and easier to harvest.

Farmers Should Not Be Prosecuted for Planting GE Seeds

Environmentalist groups and many members of Mr. da Silva's Workers' Party continue to echo European concerns about genetically modified food. They are also angry at what they call a "sell out" by Brazilian agriculture to the Monsanto Company, whose Roundup Ready technology is used in the genetically modified seeds that have entered this region from Argentina.

But at the end of the day, Mr. da Silva had little choice but to overrule such opposition, said Odacir Klein, Rio Grande's agriculture secretary. Nearly three-quarters of the state's soybean farmers have been planting the transgenic seeds for years.

While it has been technically illegal to possess genetically modified seeds, only a handful of farmers have ever been prosecuted and only minimal amounts of the seed are thought to have been seized. "Patrolling the borders is a federal task, and the previous federal government was always quietly in favor of genetically modified crops, so they never did anything, and the result was this consummated fact," Mr. Klein said.

Mr. Moreno agreed. "Even if they hadn't changed the law, we all would have planted again anyway," he said. "What could they do, arrest 150,000 of us?"

Genetically Modified Seeds Are More Effective than Traditional Crops

If Monsanto were to offer him genetically modified seeds engineered specifically for the region's climate and soil, he said he would not think twice about buying them and paying royalties to the company.

Monsanto, which has complained bitterly for years about farmers in southern Brazil using its technology but not paying royalties, welcomed the government's decree and said it hoped to find "an applicable solution" for past and future unpaid fees. That is likely to be tough going. Here, at least, farmers have stockpiled seeds from previous harvests and now do not have to smuggle seeds.

Mr. Moreno revealed a large supply of seeds stacked in his barn. "There are 2,000 bags in there," he said with a grin. "But I only need 600 bags to replant my crop."

EVALUATING THE AUTHORS' ARGUMENTS:

In this viewpoint Smith argues that genetically modified seeds do not threaten farmers but rather help them be more competitive in the agricultural marketplace. How do you think the author of the preceding viewpoint, Katherine Whitworth, might respond to this suggestion? Explain your answer using evidence from the texts.

Chapter 3

What Effects Do Genetically Modified Crops Have on the Environment?

The controversy over genetically modified crops and whether or not they are safe for the environment continues to rage.

Viewpoint

1

Genetically Modified Crops Are Environmentally Friendly

"GM could help us to grow crops with a higher yield on less land, using less water, and spraying fewer pesticides."

Olivia Judson

In the following viewpoint Olivia Judson argues that genetically modified crops are good for the environment. She challenges claims that genetically engineered crops decrease biodiversity, destroy valuable farmland, and erode the soil. On the contrary, she argues that GM crops require less land, resources, and pesticides, and thus can be described as environmentally friendly. She explains that the purpose of genetic modification is to make a better version of a plant or animal. In this way, genetic modification can make crops more water efficient or give them the ability to resist weeds and insects. The author concludes that genetically modified crops can help preserve the environment while providing food for hungry communities.

Olivia Judson, "Time to Try the Forbidden Fruit," *The Daily Telegraph* (London), March 17, 2007, p. 3. Copyright © Telegraph Media Group Limited 2007. Reproduced by permission.

Judson is an evolutionary biologist at Imperial College in London, England. She is also the copresenter of *Animal Farm*, a three-part television series on biotechnology.

AS YOU READ, CONSIDER THE FOLLOWING QUESTIONS:
1. According to the author, what is the great advantage of genetic modification?
2. Why is genetic modification more effective for making a line of water-efficient corn than selective breeding, as explained by the author?
3. What are the environmental drawbacks of organic farming, in the author's opinion?

I like genetically modified (GM) food. I'd happily tuck into a bowl of GM soy; I'd even choose it over a bowl of organic soy. I know this sounds eccentric: genetic modification is usually decried. But while much has been made of possible risks, little is made of the considerable and real benefits. Genetic modification is a useful tool that could have helpful impacts, particularly on the environment. Indeed, in my view, support for GM is a green position.

Genetic Modification Is Simple

Genetic modification sounds complicated. But actually, it's simple. There are only two things you need to know to make sense of it. The first is that a gene is a piece of DNA that contains the instructions for making a protein. Different proteins do different jobs within the body. Lactase, for example, is a protein that allows you to digest milk. The second thing you need to know is that genetic modification just means copying a gene from one organism—say, a jellyfish—and inserting it into another—perhaps a rabbit—so that the receiving organism can make a new protein.

Today [2007], genetic modification is a routine technique in laboratories around the world. Since the potential for it was discovered, 30 years ago, millions of experiments with it have been done. One of the most common modifications is to insert a jellyfish gene into something else. Why? The jellyfish *Aeguorea victoria* has a gene for a protein called green fluorescent protein. The protein glows green when you shine blue light at it. If you add the gene for green fluorescent protein to the end of some other gene, you can see when that other gene is being used: a little green light goes on. This doesn't harm the organism—and gives us a way to watch what's happening in the cell.

What's more, there's nothing preordained, or even fixed, about which organisms make which proteins. As organisms evolve, some genes fall out of use and disappear, and new ones are added. From time to time, the new ones arrive from other organisms: in other words, genes sometimes jump from one species to another. For example, the fungi that live in cows' stomachs appear to have taken their genes for digesting cellulose from bacterial co-occupants of the stomach. (Cellulose is the stuff that plants put into their cell walls; we find

Genetically modified plants have built-in pesticides and herbicides that allow farmers to use less pesticides and herbicides.

it rather indigestible). There are several ways this can happen. And when we genetically modify an organism, we mimic this jumping.

Genetic Modification Is More Efficient than Selective Breeding

The great advantage of GM is that it allows us to make precise tweaks to a plant or an animal. For thousands of years we've been doing genetic modification in a far cruder way, by selective breeding. Through this, we have created an extraordinary variety of animals and plants, taking them far beyond their natural state. From wispy grasses, we have developed new varieties of wheat and corn—impressive giants with plump kernels that we can harvest with machines. And we've bred exotica such as featherless chickens and super-muscly cows.

FAST FACT

A 2002 Council for Agricultural Science and Technology study found that genetically modified crops resulted in a 90 percent decrease in soil erosion.

Nonetheless, selective breeding is limited. Suppose you'd like to breed lines of corn that use less water. If none of your corn plants are efficient at using water, no amount of breeding will make a difference: you have to wait for the right mutations to appear. (Mutations are random changes to DNA; they occur naturally, when the DNA-copying machinery makes a mistake. However, they can also be induced.)

In the 20th century, plant scientists in the US and elsewhere began bombarding seeds with chemicals and high-energy radiation in order to cause mutations. The seeds are then grown into plants to see whether they have any useful new traits. This mutational bonanza has given us some enormous improvements in plant agriculture. But it's a crude, haphazard approach and may never succeed in generating the trait you want. Ironically, in contrast to GM, which is one of the most highly regulated processes in agriculture, this random approach is unregulated; unwanted mutants are just thrown out with the rubbish.

Genetically Engineered Food Requires Fewer Pesticides and Herbicides

Many genetically modified crops are engineered to resist bugs and weeds. As a result, they need fewer, if any, pesticides and herbicides to produce a healthy crop, and thus are viewed by some as more environmentally friendly than crops that require large amounts of pesticides and herbicides.

Product	Institution(s)	Engineered Trait(s)
Alfalfa	Monsanto	Resist glyphosate herbicide to control weeds
Canola	Bayer	Resist glufosinate herbicide to control weeds
Corn	Bayer	Resist glufosinate herbicide to control weeds/Bt toxin to control insect pests (European corn borer)
Corn	Dow/Mycogen	Bt toxin to control insect pests (corn rootworm)/ Resist glufosinate herbicide
Corn	Dow/Mycogen DuPont/Pioneer	Resist glufosinate herbicide to control weeds/Bt toxin to control insect pests (Lepidopteran)
Cotton	Monsanto	Bt toxin to control insect pests (cotton bollworms and tobacco budworm)
Cotton	Mycogen/Dow	Bt toxin to control insect pests/Resist glufosinate herbicide to control weeds
Papaya	Cornell Univ/ Univ Hawaii	Resist papaya ringspot virus
Potato	Monsanto	Bt toxin to control insect pests (Colorado potato beetle)/resist potato virus Y
Rice	Bayer	Resist glufosinate herbicide to control weeds
Soybean	Monsanto	Resist glyphosate herbicide to control weeds
Sugarbeet	Bayer	Resist glufosinate herbicide to control weeds

Taken from: United States Department of Agriculture, Environmental Protection Agency, Food and Drug Administration.

Genetically Modified Crops Can Benefit the Environment

Why bother with any of this? Like it or not, the history of agriculture is a history of beating nature: all agriculture is unnatural—has to be. Much of what occurs in nature is inedible, or meagre in quantity. The ancestor of the potato, for example, is poisonous. Moreover, growing crops in abundance is difficult. Lots of other organisms like to eat what we like. To have a harvest, a farmer has to defeat slugs, pigeons, rabbits, deer, rats, squirrels, moulds, aphids and weevils—not to mention weeds. It's remarkable that any of us has anything to eat, let alone that, in the West at least, we've made food plentiful and cheap.

We've done this by employing a variety of tools. Genetic modification is just another one. Like any tool, we can wield it well or badly. It's not a silver bullet: it won't solve all our problems. But all farming, be it organic or "industrial", is bad for the environment. All farming puts land under cultivation, erodes the soil and requires pest control.

Organic farming, indeed, takes more space than regular farming. (And here's an irony: to control pests, organic farmers often use *Bacillus thuringiensis*, a bacterium that makes a protein poisonous to insects. Inserting the gene for this protein into a plant is one of the most common genetic modifications.) GM could help us to grow crops with a higher yield on less land, using less water, and spraying fewer pesticides. Bring it on.

EVALUATING THE AUTHORS' ARGUMENTS:

The author of this viewpoint, Olivia Judson, is an evolutionary biologist at Imperial College in London. The authors of the following viewpoint, Miguel Altieri and Walter Pengue, are professors of agriculture and ecology. In other words, all are academics with expertise in the biological sciences. Given their similar backgrounds, does it surprise you that they come to different conclusions about the effect of GM crops on the environment? Explain your reasoning.

Genetically Modified Crops Are Not Environmentally Friendly

Miguel Altieri and Walter Pengue

"GM soybeans are much more environmentally damaging than other crops."

In the following viewpoint Miguel Altieri and Walter Pengue argue that genetically engineered crops are hazardous to the environment because they require extensive resources. They say that large areas of nonagricultural land—such as savannas, grasslands, and forests—are destroyed to make room for them. The many animal and plant species that live in these areas are threatened by the destruction of their habitat. Furthermore, the authors add that cultivation of genetically engineered crops deplete the soil's nutrients. To keep the soil fertile, GM crops are doused with fertilizers that eventually seep into the surrounding water supplies. Altieri and Pengue conclude that the negative effects of genetically modified crops on the environment are far reaching.

Altieri is professor of agroecology at the University of California in Berkeley.

Miguel Altieri and Walter Pengue, "GM Soybean: Latin America's new colonizer," *Seedling*, January 2006, pp. 13–17. Reproduced by permission.

He is also the author of *Genetic Engineering in Agriculture: The Myths, Environmental Risks, and Alternatives.* Pengue is professor of Agriculture and Ecology at the University of Buenos Aires in Argentina. He has written extensively on the GM soybean invasion taking place in Latin America.

AS YOU READ, CONSIDER THE FOLLOWING QUESTIONS:
1. How many hectares of nonagricultural land have been converted to soya production in Argentina, as reported by Altieri and Pengue?
2. What nontarget animals are vulnerable to the herbicide glyphosate?
3. In what two ways are genetically modified soybeans more damaging to the environment than other crops, according to the authors?

In 2005, the biotech industry and its allies celebrated the tenth consecutive year of expansion of genetically modified (GM) crops. The estimated global area of approved GM crops was 90 million hectares, a growth of 11% over the previous year. In 21 countries, they claim, GM crops have met the expectations of millions of large and small farmers in both industrialised and developing countries; delivering benefits to consumers and society at large through more affordable food, feed and fiber that are more environmentally sustainable.

Expansion of Genetically Modified Crops Destroys Land

It is hard to imagine how such expansion in GM crops has met the needs of small farmers or consumers when 60% of the global area of GM crops is devoted to herbicide-tolerant crops. In developing countries, GM crops are mostly grown for export by big farmers, not for local consumption. They are used as animal feed to produce meat consumed mostly by the wealthy.

The Latin America countries growing soybean include Argentina, Brazil, Bolivia, Paraguay and Uruguay. The expansion of soybean production is driven by prices, government and agro-industrial support, and demand from importing countries, especially China, which is the world's largest importer of soybean and soybean products. Brazil and Argentina experienced the biggest growth rates in GM soybean expansion in 2005. The expansion is accompanied by massive transportation infrastructure projects that destroy natural habitats over wide areas, well beyond the deforestation directly caused by soybean cultivation. In Brazil, soybean profits justified the improvement or construction of eight industrial waterways, three railway lines and an extensive network of roads to bring inputs and take away produce. These have attracted private investment in logging, mining, ranching and other practices that severely impact on biodiversity that have not been included in any impact assessment studies.

In Argentina, the agro-industry for transforming soybean into oils and pellets is concentrated in the Rosario region on the Parana River. This area has become the largest soy-processing estate in the world, with all the infrastructure and the environmental impact that entails. Spurred on by the export market, the Argentinean government plans further expansion of the soybean industry, adding another 4 million hectares to the existing 14 million hectares of soy production by 2010.

The area of land in soybean production in Brazil has grown on average at 3.2% or 320,000 hectares per year since 1995, resulting in a total increase of 2.3 million hectares. Today [2006] soybean occupies the largest area of any crop, covering 21% of the cultivated land. The area has increased by a factor of 57 since 1961, and production volume by a factor of 138. In Paraguay, soybeans occupy more than 25% of all agricultural land. All this expansion is at the expense of forests and other habitats. In Argentina, where 5.6 million hectares of non-agricultural land has been converted to soya production in less than ten years, forest conversion rates are three to six times the global average. In Paraguay, much of the Atlantic forest has been cut. In Brazil, the cerrado (woodland-savanna) and the grasslands are rapidly falling victim to the plow. . . .

> # FAST FACT
>
> According to scientist and researcher Charles Benbrook, farmers growing Round-up Ready soybeans in the United States used two to five times more herbicide per acre than was used on conventional crops.

What Effects Do Genetically Modified Crops Have on the Environment? 115

Soybean Cultivation Degrades the Soil

Soybean cultivation has always led to erosion, especially in areas where it is not part of a long rotation. Soil loss has reached an average rate of 16 tonnes per hectare per year (t/ha/y) in the US Midwest, far greater than is sustainable; and soil loss levels in Brazil and Argentina are estimated at between 19–30 t/ha/y depending on management, slope and climate. Farmers wrongly believe that no-till systems mean no erosion. No-till agriculture can reduce soil loss, but with the advent of herbicide tolerant soybean, many farmers now cultivate in highly erodible lands. Research shows that despite improved soil cover, erosion and negative changes in soil structure can still be substantial in highly erodible lands if weed cover is reduced.

Large-scale soybean monocultures have rendered Amazonian soils unusable. In areas of poor soils, fertilisers and lime have to be applied heavily within two years. In Bolivia, soybean production is expanding towards the east, and in many areas soils are already compacted and suffering severe soil degradation. One hundred thousand hectares of soybean-exhausted soils were abandoned for cattle-grazing, which in turn further degrades the land. As land is abandoned, farmers move to other areas where they again plant soybeans and repeat the vicious cycle of soil degradation.

In Argentina, intensive soybean cultivation has led to massive soil nutrient depletion. Continuous soybean production has extracted an estimated 1 million tonnes of nitrogen and about 227,000 tonnes of phosphorous. The estimated cost of replenishing this nutrient loss via fertilisers is US$910 million. The increased levels of nitrogen and phosphorus found in several river basins of Latin America is certainly linked to the increase of soybean production.

Genetically Modified Crops Require Toxic Herbicides

A key technical factor in the rapid spread of soybean production in Brazil was the claim that soybean's symbiotic relationship with nitrogen-fixing rhizobium bacteria in the plant's root nodules meant that the crop could be grown without fertilisers. What the companies failed to tell farmers was that the glyphosate herbicide packaged with the GM seeds is directly toxic to the bacteria, rendering the soybeans dependent on chemical fertilisers for nitrogen. Moreover, the common practice of converting uncultivated pasture to soybeans results

A Brazilian government agricultural inspector surveys transgenic soybean harvesting on a farm in Brazil in an effort to minimize potential environmental hazards of GM crops.

in an overall reduction in the levels of nitrogen-fixing bacteria, again making soybean dependent on synthetic nitrogen. . . .

Biotech companies claim that when properly applied, herbicides should not pose a threat to humans or the environment. But in practice, the large-scale planting of GM crops encourages the aerial application of herbicides and much of what is sprayed is wasted through drift and leaching. The companies contend that glyphosate degrades rapidly in the soil, does not accumulate in ground water, has no effect on non-target organisms, and leaves no residue in food, water or soil. Yet glyphosate has been reported to be toxic to some non-target species in the soil—both to beneficial predators such as spiders, mites, and carabid and coccinellid beetles, and to detritivores such as earthworms, including microfauna as well as to aquatic organisms, including fish. . . .

Moreover, research shows that glyphosate seems to act in a similar fashion to antibiotics by altering soil biology in a yet unknown way and causing effects like:

- Reducing the ability of soybeans and clover to fix nitrogen.
- Rendering bean plants more vulnerable to disease.
- Reducing growth of beneficial soil-dwelling mycorrhizal fungi, which are key for helping plants extract phosphorous from the soil.

Farm-scale evaluations in the UK showed that herbicide-resistant crop management within and in the margins of beet and oilseed rape production led to reductions in beetle, butterfly and bee populations. Counts of predacious carabid beetles that feed on weed seeds were also smaller in GM crop fields. The abundance of invertebrates that are food for mammals, birds, and other invertebrates were also found to be generally lower in herbicide-resistant beet and oilseed rape. The absence of flowering weeds in GM fields can have serious consequences for beneficial insects which require pollen and nectar for survival.

Genetically Modified Crops Damage the Environment

Soybean expansion in Latin America represents a recent and powerful threat to biodiversity in Brazil, Argentina, Paraguay and Bolivia. GM soybeans are much more environmentally damaging than other crops, partly because of their unsustainable production requirements, and partly because their export focus requires massive transportation infrastructure projects, which open up vast tracts of land to other environmentally unsound economic and extractive activities.

The production of herbicide-resistant soybean leads to environmental problems such as deforestation, soil degradation, pesticide and genetic contamination. . . .

As long as these countries continue to embrace neoliberal models of development and respond to demand from the globalised economy, the rapid proliferation of soybean will increase, and so will the associated ecological and social impacts.

EVALUATING THE AUTHORS' ARGUMENTS:

Miguel Altieri and Walter Pengue argue that genetically modified crops are dangerous to the ecology of the planet. What kinds of evidence did they use to support their claim? Did they convince you of their argument? Explain why or why not.

Genetically Modified Crops Can Help Reduce Global Warming

Derek Burke

> *"A number of approaches are needed to counter the effects of global warming [and] biofuel development is one of these."*

In the following viewpoint Derek Burke argues that genetically modified crops can be used to grow biofuel, a clean, renewable energy source that can help reduce global warming. The use of oil to power cars, industry, and homes is believed to have contributed to the warming of Earth, which scientists worry will result in a rise in ocean waters, extreme weather conditions, species extinctions, and drastic changes in crop yields. To reduce global warming, the planet is seeking a clean and renewable energy source that can power civilization as efficiently as oil does. Burke suggests turning to biofuel, which is harvested from plant material such as corn, sugar beet, oilseed rape, soy, and other sources. Some have rejected the idea of using biofuels because of constraints surrounding their growth. But Burke suggests that if biofuel plant sources

Derek Burke, "Biofuels—Is There a Role for GM?" *Biologist*, vol. 54, February 2007, pp. 52–56. Reproduced by permission.

could be genetically modified to grow very quickly on small tracts of land, they would offer an excellent fossil fuel substitute.

Derek Burke is a professor and honorary fellow of the Institute of Biology, a British organization of biologists working in industry, research, education, and health care. He is also the former chairman of the Advisory Committee on Novel Foods and Processes.

AS YOU READ, CONSIDER THE FOLLOWING QUESTIONS:
1. According to Burke, less of what would be required if genetic modification could increase the yields of oilseed rape?
2. How many gas stations does the author say will carry butanol, genetically modified beet fuel, in the UK by 2010?
3. What percent of transportation fuels does the United States want to replace with biofuels by the year 2030?

We will all agree that we face enormous challenges in dealing with the problems raised by climate change: scientific, economic and political. Nearly all of us will agree that a number of approaches are needed if we are to stabilise our world and limit the damage. One of these is the use of biofuels, for example by adding ethanol, produced by fermentation of plant biomass, to petrol for use in motor transport. . . .

Biofuels Can Reduce CO_2 Levels in the Atmosphere

Many questions are still being debated. Some ask, since there is no possibility of replacing much of Britain's fuel needs by biofuels made from crops, either grown locally or imported, why even start? How much land would be needed to have a significant effect? Does making ethanol from plant food products mean that needy people will go hungry? However, biofuels will almost certainly have a role in contributing to future fuel supplies (either to lower atmospheric CO_2 levels or to reduce our dependence on oil from unstable or unfriendly parts of the world). So what should we be doing in Britain? . . .

Apart from the economic and political problems that lie ahead for biofuels, there are a number of scientific hurdles to overcome, such as increasing the productivity per acre and increasing the biofuel transformation efficiency, thereby reducing the cost of production and furthering sustainable development. Can biotechnology, including genetic modification, play any useful role here? . . .

If the development of GM biofuels rekindles interest in plant biology and plant genetics, so much the better. Though badly wounded, plant science is not yet dead in Britain, and could be revived if given a measure of encouragement and protection from ideological vandalism and attack. In time, morale would improve and commercial companies might even bring back some of their research laboratories.

There are several key issues. First, are there suitable genetically modified crops which might be grown in the UK? Two crops merit careful consideration: oilseed rape and sugar beet.

Genetically Modified Fuel

As oil prices rise, experts are considering whether ethanol, a fuel derived from corn, grass, and other crops could eventually replace gasoline. Genetically modified seeds could allow larger crops to grow faster, resulting in more plants from which to make ethanol fuel. The following chart is one engineer's guess of how genetic engineering technology will allow corn and other biofuel crops to become a popular energy source for America.

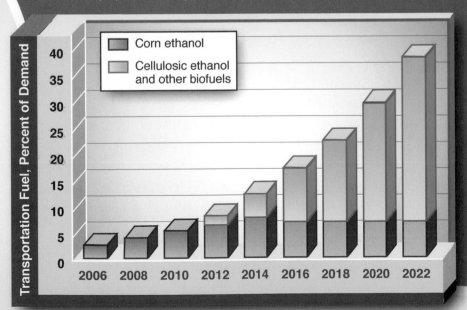

Taken from: Vinod Khosla, "Biofuels Trajectory to Success: The Innovation Ecosystem at Work," Khosla Ventures, 2007. www.khoslaventures.com/presentation/BiofuelsPathways.pdf.

Oilseed Rape Yields More on Less Land

A back-of-the-envelope calculation on how much more oilseed rape is required to achieve the 5% inclusion rate into diesel fuel already committed to by the Government last year, suggests around 500,000 hectares—or almost double what is currently grown. Discussions with agronomists suggest that this is possible although difficult, since it would require oilseed rape to be grown more often in a rotation. Currently oilseed rape is grown once every 3–5 years on a typical field to avoid problems such as club root and other brassica diseases. To get the required amount of oilseed rape grown in the UK, the rotation would have to be compressed to 2–3 years, with all the associated disease problems.

FAST FACT

Genetically modified crops reduce greenhouse gas emissions from farm equipment and machinery by 85 percent, according to a 2002 Council for Agricultural Science and Technology study.

However, if it were possible to radically increase yields of oilseed rape, less land would be required. The non-optimised GM oilseed rape varieties trialled in the UK a couple of years ago increased yield by an average of 14%. At that sort of increase, achieving the fuel obligation with raw materials sourced in the UK is well within the realms of possibilities. This could help the farmer as well as providing an environmental benefit. . . .

Genetic Modification of the Sugar Beet Is Good for the Environment

GM glyphosate-tolerant sugar beet is a good example of the substantial benefit arising from genetic modification of a potential biofuel crop—for a number of reasons. First, it offers a substantial economic advantage. Approximately 10% (£2/ tonne) reduction in the production cost of beet is attainable, due roughly equally to reduced input costs (herbicides) and increased yield (absence of phytotoxicity).

Second, the direct ecotoxicity profile of glyphosate is extremely favourable and there is a marked reduction in overall herbicide use.

Oilseed rape, like this crop shown in the United Kingdom, is a crop that many experts think can be economically converted to biofuel.

Crop management strategies have been developed to mitigate any adverse effects on farmland biodiversity. There is no longer any rational case why this particular GM crop need have any adverse environmental impact in the UK farmland. Indeed, it could be managed to be more favourable to farmland birds than the conventional crop, whilst maintaining most of its economic advantage.

Third, the conventional sugar beet crop is declining in area and under severe economic pressure due to European sugar regime reform. Retention of spring crops is important to retain landscape diversity, with its associated ecological benefits, in a UK farmland landscape nowadays dominated by autumn crops. An economically viable GM herbicide-tolerant sugar beet crop for biofuel could make an important contribution to the UK landscape.

These benefits can only be realised if industry is prepared to exploit beet as a biofuel. The current situation in the UK is that the first biobutanol plant is being built near Downham Market in Norfolk by BP, Du Pont and British Sugar and is designed to produce 70 million litres of fuel a year, using beet surplus to quota. Butanol is expected to be introduced in all 1250 BP filling stations by 2010. Any larger scale development is predicated on wheat as the feedstock. However, such a development would exacerbate problems of autumn crops dominating the landscape and would compete directly with the forecast increasing global food demand in the medium term. With two existing sugar factories about to close, it is regrettable that there is not an opportunity to respond to the medium term economic scenario. Development of a biofuel industry would also change the design of any future beet processing plants. . . .

Genetically Modified Biofuels Are an Alternative to Fossil Fuels

The US Department of Energy (DOE) has announced that it will invest US $250 million to establish and run two Bioenergy Research Centers for the development of biofuels. The centres will conduct systems biology research on micro-organisms and plants, with the aim of harnessing and improving on nature's own ways of producing energy from sunlight. "This is an important step toward our goal of replacing 30% of transportation fuels with biofuels by 2030," said Secretary Samuel Bodman. "The mission of these centres is to accelerate research that leads to breakthroughs in basic science to make biofuels a cost-effective alternative to fossil fuels." Public and private research institutions are eligible to compete for an award to establish and operate a centre. They are expected to open in 2008 and be fully operational by 2009.

In the USA, Monsanto are major suppliers of *Processor Preferred* corn varieties for the rapidly-growing fuel ethanol industry, which now produces over 4.3 billion gallons of fuel ethanol annually. In addition, Sandia National Laboratories and Monsanto Company recently announced a three-year research collaboration that is aimed at aligning Sandia's capabilities in bioanalytical imaging and analysis with Monsanto's research in developing new seed-based products for farmers, including corn products that may be able to produce more ethanol per bushel. . . .

Global Warming Can Be Reduced by Genetically Modified Crops

It is generally agreed that a number of approaches are needed to counter the effects of global warming, that biofuel development is one of these, and that scientific and technical advances are needed to make such an approach viable. Other reviews have discussed problems and opportunities, but none has considered the advantages of using GM crops such as GM rape and GM sugar beet as sources of biofuels. Any environmental problems could be contained and there are no human health issues. But could such use of genetic modification escape the stigma that it has so inappropriately (in my view) collected? Is the British public now ready to consider the benefits of such an approach? I hope so, and then the deciding factor will be the outcome of an economic cost/benefit analysis.

EVALUATING THE AUTHOR'S ARGUMENTS:

Burke argues that genetically modified biofuels like oilseed rape and sugar beet can be used to reduce global warming. What do you think? Can the development of genetically modified crops replace traditional fossil fuels in enough time to reverse the damage caused by global warming? And if they could, is their impact on the environment worth it? Explain your position.

Genetically Modified Crops Cannot Reduce Global Warming

Mark Lynas

"It is stretching credulity to argue that biofuels produced through deforestation are helping combat climate change."

In the following viewpoint Mark Lynas argues that global warming cannot be reduced using genetically modified biofuel crops. He explains that the production of biofuels is an environmental threat in itself: Fires are often used to clear land to grow genetically modified biofuel crops, resulting in the release of high quantities of carbon dioxide, which further contribute to global warming. In addition, fossil fuels—a main culprit of global warming—are used throughout most stages of biofuel manufacture. The author concludes that the government's plan to reduce global warming with genetically modified biofuel crops is just a gimmick that takes the focus away from the real threat of global warming.

Mark Lynas, "Frankenstein Fuels," *New Statesman*, vol. 135, August 7, 2006, pp. 30–31. Copyright © 2006 New Statesman, Ltd. Reproduced by permission.

Lynas has worked for nearly a decade as a specialist on climate change and is the author of three books on the subject: *High Tide: News from a Warming World*, *Carbon Calculator*, and *Six Degrees: Our Future on a Hotter Planet*.

AS YOU READ, CONSIDER THE FOLLOWING QUESTIONS:
1. How many tons of carbon dioxide were released by burning land to grow palm oil biofuel, as reported by the author?
2. According to Lynas, ethanol takes how much more energy to make than the fuel itself offers?
3. What reason does the author give for the government's investment in biofuels?

L ate every summer, large areas of central Borneo become invisible. There's no magic involved—most of the densely forested island simply gets covered with a pall of thick smoke. Huge areas of forest burn, while beneath the ground peat many metres thick smoulders on for months. These trees are burning in a good cause, however. They are burning to help save the world from global warming.

Here is how the logic goes. As the natural forest is cleared, land opens up for lucrative palm-oil plantations. Palm oil is a feedstock for biodiesel, the "carbon-neutral" fuel that the European Union [EU] is trying to encourage by converting its vehicle fleet. By reducing use of fossil fuels for its cars and trucks, the EU believes it can reduce its carbon emissions and thereby help mitigate global warming. Everyone is happy. (Except the orang-utan. It gets to go extinct.)

It's a con, of course. In 1997, the single worst year of Indonesian forest- and peat-burning, 2.67 billion tonnes of carbon dioxide were released by the fires, equivalent to 40 per cent of the year's entire emissions from burning fossil fuels. That was a particularly bad year: most summers, the emissions are only a billion or so tonnes, or about 15 per cent of total human emissions. The biggest Indonesian fires, in 1997 and 1998, took place on plantation company land, while in neighbouring Malaysia 87 per cent of recent deforestation has occurred to make way for palm-oil plantations. It is stretching credulity to argue that biofuels produced through this destructive process are helping combat climate change.

Genetically Modified Biofuels Attract Big Business

The EU is undaunted (though it has undertaken a public consultation), and persists with a target that 5.75 per cent of its vehicle fuels should be "renewable" by the year 2010. Not all of this will come from tropical sources such as palm oil—but nor can their importation be restricted on environmental grounds. The campaigning journalist George Monbiot has discovered that world trade rules would prevent the EU taking any measures to restrict imports of palm oil produced on deforested lands. Free trade comes first. . . .

As the promise of profits increases, the big players are beginning to get involved. The two largest external stakes in Greenergy Biofuels are held by Tesco and Cargill. Tesco will shift the product on its petrol forecourts, while Cargill—one of two giants that dominate the world food market—will supply the feedstock. Gone are the days when biofuels meant bearded hippies running their clapped-out vans on recycled chip fat.

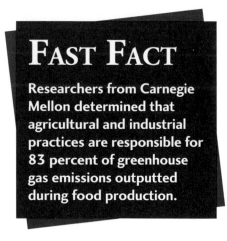

FAST FACT

Researchers from Carnegie Mellon determined that agricultural and industrial practices are responsible for 83 percent of greenhouse gas emissions outputted during food production.

Even the oil majors are sniffing around this new market. BP has teamed up with DuPont to develop a liquid fuel called biobutanol, derived from sugar cane or corn starch, which they aim to launch in the UK [United Kingdom] next year as an additive to petrol. In the meantime, the oil giant is ploughing half a billion dollars into biofuels research at a new academic laboratory called the Energy Biosciences Institute. Indeed, "biosciences" are what it's all about. Speak to anyone in the corporate energy or agricultural sectors and they will probably go dewy-eyed about the technological "convergence" of energy, food, genetics—in fact, just about everything. In the biotechnology industry the atmosphere is reminiscent of the heady days of genetic modification, before the companies realised that consumers didn't want to eat "Frankenstein foods". Frankenstein fuels, however, might prove an easier sell.

An ethanol plant is shown under construction in Missouri. Some people think that making food crops into fuel for cars is not necessarily a good idea while global harvest yields are declining.

Genetically Modified Crop Industry Using Climate Change to Attract Interest

The GM industry now plans to reinvent itself, following the example of the nuclear industry, on the back of climate change. "Producing genetically modified crops for non-food purposes, as a renewable source of alternative fuels, may provide the basis for a more rational and balanced consideration of the technology and its potential benefits, away from the disproportionate hysteria which has so often accompanied the debate over GM foods," suggests the Agricultural Biotechnology Council, an umbrella organisation for the biggest biotech companies. The Swiss corporation Syngenta is already marketing a variety of GM corn—one not approved for human consumption or animal feed—specifically intended for ethanol biofuels. It has just applied, with support from the UK, for an EU import licence—even though it admits it "cannot exclude" the possibility that some of this corn will find its way into the normal supply chain. The European biotech association EuropaBio is delighted with the EU's biofuels initiative. "Biotechnology will help to meet Europe's carbon-dioxide emission reduction targets, reduce our dependence on oil imports and provide another useful income stream for our farmers," enthuses its secretary general, Johan Vanhemelrijck.

In the United States, biofuels are welcomed as a way to help wean the country off its dependence on oil produced by shady, Allah-obsessed Arabs. "Every gallon of renewable, domestically produced fuel we use is a gallon we don't have to get from other countries," beams Congressman Kenny Hulshof, a Republican sponsor of the Renewable Fuels and Energy Independence Promotion Act being considered by Congress. Not surprisingly, the American Soybean Association is also a supporter. "ASA is urging all soybean growers to contact their members of Congress and ask them to co-sponsor this legislation," says its president, Bob Metz, in a press release. . . .

In America, biofuels combine patriotism with economic self-interest in a seamless match. Farmers love it because biodiesel and ethanol are brewed from agricultural commodities, helping drive up farm-gate prices. Red-state senators love it because federal tax subsidies keep Republican voting farmers happy. Even George W. Bush loves it: "I like the idea of a policy that combines agriculture and modern science with the energy needs of the American people," the president told the Renewable Fuels Association in April [2006].

Democrats and Republicans are united in touting ethanol. "All incumbents and challengers in Midwestern farm country are by definition ethanolics," the agricultural policy adviser Ken Cook told the *New York Times.* There are 40 ethanol plants under construction, and the US is poised to overtake Brazil (which uses sugar cane on a large scale to make the fuel) as the world's largest producer within a year. Cargill's CEO compares the transformation to "a gold rush".

Biofuels Still Rely on Fossil Fuels

But not everybody loves biofuels. David Pimentel, professor of insect ecology and agriculture at Cornell University, hates them. "There is just no energy benefit to using plant biomass for liquid fuel," he complains. Pimentel's own studies have concluded that making ethanol from corn uses 30 per cent more energy than the finished fuel produces, because fossil fuels are used at every stage in the production process, from cultivation (in fertilisers) to transportation. "Abusing our precious croplands to grow corn for an energy-inefficient process that yields lowgrade automobile fuel amounts to unsustainable, subsidised food burning," he fumes.

Pimentel is not alone in thinking that burning food in cars while global harvests decline is not necessarily a good idea. China, with its enormous population, is already having second thoughts about going down the biofuels path. "Basically this country has such a large population that the top priority for land use is food crops," says Dr. Sergio Trindade, an expert on biofuels. The same problem will doubtless hamper the biofuels revolution in Europe. According to one study, meeting the EU's 5.75 per cent target for its vehicles will require about a quarter of Europe's agricultural land. For the even more car-dependent US, it would take 1.8 billion acres of farmland—four times the country's total arable area—to produce enough soya biodiesel to cover annual petrol consumption.

Genetically Modified Crops Do Not Reduce Emissions

So which gets priority: cars or people? A very simple answer to this land/fuel conundrum would be for people to use their cars less, and to cycle and walk more. But discouraging car use is not at the top of any politician's agenda, either in Europe or the US. Meanwhile, our leaders must be seen to be doing something about the rising greenhouse-gas emissions from road transport, so biofuels are the perfect technofix.

The dilemma might bring to mind Douglas Adams's [book] *Hitchhiker's Guide to the Galaxy*, where the alien Ford Prefect took the name of a car because—looking down from above at all the busy roads and motorways—he had mistaken them for the dominant life form. If cars chug happily around between massed ranks of starving people in our biofuelled future, then perhaps Ford Prefect won't have got it so wrong after all.

EVALUATING THE AUTHOR'S ARGUMENTS:

Mark Lynas quotes from several sources to support the points in his essay. Make a list of everyone he quotes, including their credentials and the nature of their comments. Then, analyze his sources—are they credible? Are they well qualified to speak on the subject?

Facts About Genetically Modified Food

Editors' note: These facts can be used in reports or papers to reinforce or add credibility when making important points or claims.

Genetically Modified Foods and the United States
- Approximately two-thirds of processed foods contain a genetically engineered organism.
- According to the Food Institute, over 70 percent of processed products on grocery shelves contain genetically engineered ingredients designed mainly to ward off pests and withstand herbicides.
- Since their introduction in 1996, GM foods have become abundant throughout the United States. Genetically engineered crops account for about 89 percent of the soybeans, 61 percent of the corn, and 83 percent of the cotton grown in the United States.
- Currently, no U.S. laws state foods that contain genetically modified organisms must be labeled.
- The United States leads the world in the planting of biotech crops, with more than 96 million acres of genetically modified crop seeds planted.
- In 2006 the United States grew 53 percent of almost all transgenic crops.
- The U.S. Department of Agriculture lists a number of crops that have genetically modified versions:
  - soybeans
  - corn
  - cotton
  - tomatoes
  - rapeseed plants
  - sugar cane
  - sweet corn
  - rice

Genetically Modified Food Around the World
- According to the International Service of Agri-Biotech Applications, more than 27 percent of the world's genetically engineered crops are located in developing countries.

- Opponents of genetically modified seeds often argue that a food shortage is not necessarily responsible for hunger. India, for example, is the third largest producer of food in the world, producing from 40 to 80 million tons of excess food grains in a year, yet over 350 million Indians are starving.
- Almost 78 percent of countries with serious child malnutrition problems are food-exporting countries—meaning the food they produce is traded to other countries instead of feeding their own people.
- Under current European Union (EU) law, products such as ketchup, cooking oil, and cake mix must be labeled if the ingredients include 0.9 percent or more genetically modified organisms (GMO).
- Greenpeace claims up to 30 percent of an animal's diet contains GMOs, and 90 percent of genetically modified crops imported into the EU are soy and corn destined for animal feed.
- Soybeans, corn, cotton, and canola are the main genetically modified crops planted around the world:
  - 63 percent of biotech plantings are soybean crops.
  - 19 percent of biotech plantings are corn crops.
  - 13 percent of biotech plantings are cotton crops.
  - 5 percent of biotech plantings are canola crops.
- Argentina has 13.4 million acres of biotech crops.
- Canada has 8.6 million acres of biotech crops.
- China has 5.2 million acres of biotech crops.
- In 2006, 44 percent of genetically modified crops came from Argentina (17 percent), Brazil (11 percent), Canada (6 percent), India (4 percent), China (3 percent), Paraguay (2 percent) and South Africa (1 percent).
- The following nations have 1 million or fewer acres of biotech crops: Australia, Bulgaria, Colombia, Germany, Honduras, India, Indonesia, Mexico, Romania, South Africa, and Uruguay.
- A 2003 survey by the Pew Research Center found that 63 percent of Canadians, 81 percent of Germans, and 89 percent of French people disapprove of GM foods.

Genetically Modified Foods and Human Health
- According to the World Health Organization (WHO), several potential risks to human consumption of genetically modified foods include:
  - toxicity
  - allergic reactions

- instability of inserted gene
- nutritional effects associated with genetic modification
- unintended effects caused by gene insertion

- The Seeds of Deception Web site cites the following studies and occurrences as evidence of the harmful reaction to genetically engineered organisms in animals and humans:
  - Rats fed GMO tomatoes got bleeding stomachs, several died.
  - Rats fed Bt corn had multiple health problems.
  - Mice fed Bt potatoes had intestinal damage.
  - Workers exposed to Bt cotton developed allergies.
  - Sheep died after grazing in Bt cotton fields.
  - Inhaled Bt corn pollen may have triggered disease in humans.
  - Farmers report pigs and cows became sterile from GM corn.
  - Twelve cows in Germany died after being fed Bt corn.
  - Mice fed Roundup Ready soy had liver cell problems.
  - Mice fed Roundup Ready soy had problems with the pancreas.
  - Mice fed Roundup Ready soy had unexplained changes in testicular cells.
  - Roundup Ready soy changed cell metabolism in rabbit organs.
  - Most offspring of rats fed Roundup Ready soy died within three weeks.
  - Soy allergies skyrocketed in the UK soon after GM soy was introduced.
  - GM peas generated an allergic-type inflammatory response in mice.

- An independent report published by the UK in 2003 revealed "no verifiable untoward toxic or nutritionally deleterious effects" from the worldwide consumption of GM foods by humans and livestock over the last seven years. It also found no compelling evidence that humans who eat GM food absorb bacteria from the plants into the stomach.
- In 1992 the FDA published guidelines to ensure that biotechnology companies worked with the FDA in assessing the safety of genetically modified foods for human consumption. Companies must test the safety of their products and submit their results to the FDA for evaluation.
- As of April 2002, fifty products had been submitted to the FDA, and most of those were approved for human consumption.

Testing up to this point has been voluntary and not mandated by law.

GM Foods and the Environment

- The World Health Organization recognizes a number of environmental concerns when addressing genetically engineered crops:
  - the potential of a genetically modified organism introducing engineered genes into wild populations,
  - the persistence of the gene after the GMO has been harvested,
  - the loss of biodiversity in plants and wildlife,
  - increased use of chemicals in agriculture,
  - the detrimental effect on non-pest insects,
  - potential for the development of new plant pathogens,
  - decreased use of crop rotation in certain local situations that depend upon it, and
  - movement of herbicide resistance of GM plants to other crops.
- A 2002 Council for Agricultural Science and Technology found that genetically modified crops are good for the environment, resulting in:
  - the adoption of conservation farming techniques,
  - the preservation of 37 million tons of topsoil,
  - an 85 percent reduction in greenhouse gas emissions from farm equipment and machinery,
  - a 70 percent reduction in herbicide runoff, and
  - a 90 percent decrease in soil erosion.
- A plant can cross-pollinate with another plant from a related species located as far as three kilometers away, according to the Council for Responsible Genetics. This could mean that genetically modified seeds could pollute crops that are miles away.
- According to the USDA, biotechnology provides farmers with tools that can make food production less expensive and more manageable than growing traditional crops. Some examples include:
  - biotechnology crops that can be engineered to tolerate specific herbicides, which makes weed control simpler and more efficient;
  - other crops that have been engineered to be resistant to specific plant diseases and insect pests, which can make pest control more reliable and effective and/or can decrease the use of synthetic pesticides.

Genetically Modified Food and the Future

- There is great potential for "functional foods"—foods that provide health benefits beyond basic nutrition—to be developed in the future. According to the USDA, future advances in biotechnology may provide consumers with the following benefits:
  - nutritionally enriched food
  - foods that are longer lasting or have a longer shelf life
  - foods with lower levels of certain naturally occurring toxins present in some food plants
  - reduced allergens in foods
  - increased disease-fighting nutrients in foods
  - oils that produce no trans fats or contain heart healthy omega-3 fatty acids
  - cassava with increased protein content to help fight malnutrition in developing nations
  - foods with enhanced levels of antioxidants to fight cancers
- Genetically engineered plants are also being developed for a purpose known as phytoremediation. This means plants would be able to detoxify pollutants in the soil or absorb and accumulate polluting substances out of the soil. In either case the result is improved soil quality at a polluted site.
- Biotechnology may also be used to conserve natural resources in the future. Animals would be able to more effectively use nutrients present in feed, thereby decreasing the amount of food necessary to feed them. Nutrient runoff into rivers and bays would decrease, which would help meet the increasing world food and land demands. Researchers also aim to develop hardier crops that will flourish in even the harshest environments and that will require less fuel, labor, fertilizer, and water, and subsequently help to decrease the pressures on land and wildlife habitats.

Glossary

allergen: A substance that causes an allergic reaction.

allergy: A hypersensitivity to an allergen or substance in a person's environment such as dust, pollen, fur, food, or a chemical.

biodiversity: Refers to the variety of ecosystems and plant and animal species that can be found in the environment.

biotechnology: The use of living things to make or change products (such as food products).

Bt crops: Bt stands for *Bacillus thuringiensis,* a soil-based bacterium that makes a toxin lethal to insect pests. The Bt-toxin gene can be "engineered" into plants (such as Bt cotton) to kill specific insects.

chromosome: A long thread of nucleic acids and protein found in the nucleus of most living cells. Chromosomes carry genetic information in the form of genes.

deoxyribonucleic acid (DNA): An organism's storehouse of biological information and the carrier of hereditary information.

ecology: The study of the interrelations between living things and their environment.

ecosystem: A biological community of interacting organisms and their physical environment.

food chain: Encompasses the whole process of food production from the fields of the farmer and the food their animals eat to food manufacturing, processing, distribution, and to the dinner table.

gene: A portion of a chromosome (DNA) that contains the hereditary information or particular characteristics of a living organism.

gene technology: A branch of modern biotechnology that attempts to control or modify genes, by moving them between two unrelated species (called recombinant DNA technology).

genetically modified foods: Any food containing parts of genetically modified plants, animals, or microorganisms.

genetically modified organism (GMO): Any plant, animal, micro-organism or virus that has been genetically altered by the addition of foreign genes to enhance a desired trait.

genetic diversity: The total of genetic information, contained in the genes of all the plants, animals, and microorganisms that live on Earth.

genetic engineering: The deliberate modification of the characteristics of an organism by manipulating its genetic material (DNA/genes).

genetics: The study of heredity and the variation of inherited character-istics (or the genetic properties or features of an organism).

genome: An organism's total DNA.

herbicide: A weed killer used in crop production.

herbicide-tolerant/resistant crops: Plants genetically engineered to tol-erate herbicides used to kill weeds.

insect-resistant plants: Plants resistant to certain insect pests, through a built-in insecticide.

Monsanto: A transnational corporation that markets a huge range of farming products, with a particular focus on agricultural biotechnology.

organic farming: Farming that uses soil free of synthetic chemicals and fertilizers.

organism: An individual animal, plant, or single-celled life form.

pesticide: A toxic chemical substance sprayed onto crops to prevent dam-age by insects.

precautionary principle: The key principle of ecologically sustainable development: When lack of scientific certainty and possibility of serious or irreversible damage to the environment exist, society should recognize this uncertainty and put in place measures that will avoid possible damage.

recombinant DNA technology: The technology that allows the transfer of already existing genes from one organism to another with special car-riers or vectors, such as bacteria and viruses.

segregation: When genetically modified crops are kept separate from conventional crops.

superpest: A plant pest that has developed a resistance to an insecticide it was once intolerant of.

superweed: A weed that has developed a resistance to a herbicide that once destroyed it.

sustainability: A holistic approach that aims at preserving the environment's natural and nonrenewable resources (soil and water). Sustainable agricultural systems are considered to be ecologically sound, economically viable, socially just, and humane.

terminator gene: A patented gene technology that modifies plants so that they become sterile and the seed by the parent crop does not grow. This means the seed cannot be saved and grown by the farmer the next year.

transgenic: Used to describe plants and animals that have been genetically engineered to contain the genes from another species, such as from a virus, animal, or plant.

virus-resistant plants: Plants that have been genetically modified so that they are resistant to a particular disease-causing virus.

Organizations to Contact

The editors have compiled the following list of organizations concerned with the issues debated in this book. The descriptions are derived from materials provided by the organizations. All have publications or information available for interested readers. The list was compiled on the date of publication of the present volume; the information provided here may change. Be aware that many organizations take several weeks or longer to respond to inquiries, so allow as much time as possible.

Alliance for Bio-Integrity
2040 Pearl Ln., Ste. 2
Fairfield, IA 52556
(206) 888-4852
e-mail:info@biointegrity.org
Web site: www.biointegrity.org

The Alliance for Bio-Integrity is a nonprofit organization that opposes the use of genetic engineering in agriculture and works to educate the public about the dangers of genetically modified foods. Articles that argue against genetic engineering from legal, religious, and scientific perspectives—including "Why Concerns About Health Risks of Genetically Engineered Food Are Scientifically Justified"—can be found on its Web site.

Biotechnology Industry Organization (BIO)
1201 Maryland Ave. SW, Ste. 900
Washington, DC 20024
(202) 962-9200
fax: (202) 488-6301
e-mail: info@bio.org
Web site: www.bio.org

BIO represents biotechnology companies, academic institutions, state biotechnology centers, and related organizations that support the use of biotechnology in improving health care, agriculture, efforts to clean up the environment, and other fields. BIO publishes fact sheets, background-ers, and position papers on various issues related to genetic engineering, including "Facts and Fiction About Plant and Animal Biotechnology."

Center for Food Safety (CFS)
660 Pennsylvania Ave. SE, #302
Washington, DC 20003
(202) 547-9359
fax: (202) 547-9429
e-mail: office@centerforfoodsafety.org
Web site: www.centerforfoodsafety.org

The CFS is a nonprofit public interest organization that works to pro-tect human health and the environment by challenging harmful food production technologies and promoting organic and sustainable alter-natives. It offers legal, scientific, and grassroots support to citizens and organizations concerned with food safety and sustainable agriculture. It reports on its recent work in its quarterly newsletter *Food Safety Now!* and provides in-depth analysis of food safety topics in its *Food Safety Review* publications.

Council for Biotechnology Information
1201 Maryland Ave. SW, Ste. 400
Washington, DC 20024
(202) 962-9200
Web site: http://whybiotech.com

The council is an organization made up of biotechnology companies and trade associations. Its purpose is to promote the benefits of bio-technology in agriculture, industry, science, and health care. Its Web site offers numerous reports and FAQs on various topics, including the economic and environmental impact of genetically engineered crops.

Council for Responsible Genetics (CRG)
5 Upland Rd., Ste. 3
Cambridge, MA 02140
(617) 868-0870
fax: (617) 491-5344
e-mail: crg@gene-watch.org
Web site: www.gene-watch.org

CRG is a national nonprofit organization of scientists, public health advocates, and others who promote a comprehensive public interest agenda for biotechnology. Its members work to raise public awareness about genetic discrimination, patenting life forms, food safety, and environmental quality. CRG publishes *Gene Watch* magazine and provides access to current and archived articles on its Web site.

Food and Drug Administration (FDA)
5600 Fishers Ln.
Rockville, MD 20857
(888) 463-6332
e-mail: webmail@oc.fda.gov
Web site: www.fda.gov

The FDA is a public health agency that protects American consumers by enforcing the Federal Food, Drug, and Cosmetic Act and several related public health laws. The FDA ensures the safety of the U.S. food supply and enforces labeling of products. It also provides the public with accurate and science-based information through its government documents, reports, fact sheets, and press announcements.

Food First/Institute for Food and Development Policy
398 Sixtieth St.
Oakland, CA 94618
(510) 654-4400
fax: (510) 654-4551
e-mail: info@foodfirst.org
Web site: www.foodfirst.org

The Institute for Food and Development Policy is a think tank that works to end hunger, poverty, and environmental degradation around the world. The goal of ending world hunger is promoted through research, analysis, advocacy, and education with the aim of securing people's right to healthy food produced through ecologically sound methods. The institute works to protect indigenous communities threatened by the expansion of genetically modified crops.

Foundation on Economic Trends (FOET)
4520 East West Hwy., Ste. 600
Bethesda, MD 20814

(301) 656-6272
fax: (301) 654-0208
e-mail: jrifkin@foet.org
Web site: www.foet.org

Founded by science critic and author Jeremy Rifkin, the foundation is a nonprofit organization whose mission is to examine emerging trends in science and technology and their impacts on the environment, the economy, culture, and society. FOET works to educate the public about topics such as gene patenting, commercial eugenics, genetic discrimination, and genetically altered food. Its Web site contains news updates and articles, including "Shopping for Humans" and "Unknown Risks of Genetically Engineered Crops."

Friends of the Earth (FOE)

1717 Massachusetts Ave. NW, Ste. 600
Washington, DC 20036-2002
(877) 843-8687
fax: (202) 783-0444
e-mail: foe@foe.org
Web site: www.foe.org

Founded in San Francisco in 1969 by David Brower, Friends of the Earth is a grassroots organization whose goal is to create a healthier, more just world. FOE members founded the world's largest federation of democratically elected environmental groups, Friends of the Earth International. Among other efforts, FOE conducted lab tests confirming that genetically engineered corn not approved for human consumption was in products on supermarket shelves across the nation. Current and archived issues of its quarterly newsmagazine *Friends of the Earth* are available on its Web site.

Institute for Agriculture and Trade Policy (IATP)

2105 First Ave. South
Minneapolis, MN 55404
(612) 870-0453
fax: (612) 870-4846
e-mail: iatp@iatp.org

The IATP is an organization that works to ensure fair and sustainable food, farm, and trade systems both locally and globally. The IATP monitors the impact of genetically engineered crops on the environment, human health, and farmer income. It maintains the Genetically Engineered Food Alert (GEFA) Web site, which provides visitors with information about genetically engineered food, food safety, and food security.

Institute for Responsible Technology (IRT)
(641) 209-1765
e-mail: info@responsibletechnology.org
Web site: www.responsibletechnology.org

The IRT is an online community of scientists and leaders who aim to eradicate genetically modified organisms from the world's food supply. By using grassroots and national strategies the IRT educates the public about the dangerous health effects of GM foods and fights for public policies that will protect consumers from GM technology.

Organic Consumers Association (OCA)
6771 S. Silver Hill Dr.
Finland, MN 55603
(218) 226-4164
fax: (218) 353-7652
www.organicconsumers.org

The OCA is an online and grassroots nonprofit organization that represents organic, family farm, and environmental businesses in critical issues, including food safety, industrial agriculture, genetic engineering, and environmental sustainability. The OCA challenges industrial agriculture and promotes buying locally, fair-made, organic products through its public education and network-building programs such as the Breaking the Chains campaign. It publishes a biweekly e-mail publication called *Organic Bytes*, and its Web site provides many articles on genetically modified foods.

Secretariat of the Convention on Biological Diversity
413 Saint Jacques St., Ste. 300
Montreal, QC H2Y 1N9, Canada
(514) 288-2220
fax: (514) 288-6588
e-mail: secretariat@cbd.int
Web site: www.cbd.int

The Secretariat of the Convention on Biological Diversity promotes scientific cooperation among the signatories of the 1992 biodiversity treaty. It produces newsletters and brochures, and its Web site disseminates numerous documents and studies pertaining to biodiversity.

U.S. Department of Agriculture (USDA)

1400 Independence Ave. SW
Washington, DC 20250
e-mail: agsec@usda.gov
Web site: www.usda.gov
Web site on agricultural biotechnology: www.nal.usda.gov/bic

The USDA is one of three federal agencies primarily responsible for regulating biotechnology in the United States. Its Animal and Plant Health Inspection Service (APHIS) division regulates the introduction of genetically engineered organisms into the environment that may pose a risk to plant or animal health. The USDA conducts research on the safety of genetically engineered organisms, helps form government policy on agricultural biotechnology, and provides information to the public about these technologies.

For Further Reading

Books

Avise, John C. *The Hope, Hype, and Reality of Genetic Engineering: Remarkable Stories from Agriculture, Industry, Medicine, and the Environment.* New York: Oxford University Press, 2004. An objective examination of fifty genetic engineering projects and the successes and failures surrounding each.

Cummings, Claire Hope. *Uncertain Peril: Genetic Engineering and the Future of Seeds.* Boston: Beacon, 2008. Presents a stark portrait of how Earth's ecology and food supply are threatened by genetically modified seeds.

Harrison, Beth H. *Shedding Light on Genetically Engineered Food: What You Don't Know About the Food You're Eating and What You Can Do to Protect Yourself.* Bloomington, IN: iUniverse, 2007. Argues that genetically modified food is not safe for human consumption and questions the biotechnology industry's role in distributing potentially harmful products to consumers.

Kimbrell, Andrew. *Your Right to Know: Genetic Engineering and the Secret Changes in Your Food.* San Rafael, CA: Earth Aware, 2007. A historical reference as well as a collection of interviews with scientists, farmers, and doctors discussing how genetic engineering impacts human food consumption.

Nottingham, Stephen. *Eat Your Genes: How Genetically Modified Food Is Entering Our Diet.* London: Zed, 2003. Argues that the promises of genetic engineering are not being met and discusses the potential ecological and health risks of genetically modified crops and livestock.

Ronald, Pamela C., and R.W. Adamchak. *Tomorrow's Table: Organic Farming, Genetics, and the Future of Food.* New York: Oxford University Press, 2008. Argues that a blend of organic farming and genetic engineering is the best way to help feed the world's growing population.

Thomson, Jennifer A. *Seeds for the Future: The Impact of Genetically Modified Crops on the Environment.* New York: Cornell University

Press, 2007. A quantitative study that determines the benefits of GM crops outweigh the risks and that evidence that GM crops are harmful to the environment does not exist.

Periodicals and Internet Sources

Allen, Kimberly Jordan. "Edible History: Discovering the Benefits of Heirloom Fruits and Vegetables (Eating Right)," *E*, May/June 2005.

Bangkok Post. "GM Rice No Solution to Poverty and Starvation," October 17, 2005.

Business Week Online. "Online Extra: Salmon That Grow Up Fast; if Elliot Entis Can Win FDA Approval for His Quick-Growing Fish, He'll Pave the Way for Other Food Companies Working on Genetically Modified Animals," January 11, 2006.

Cohen, Joel. "Poorer Nations Turn to Publicly Developed GM Crops," *Nature Biotechnology*, January 2005.

Coleman, Gerald D. "Is Genetic Engineering the Answer to Hunger?" *America*, February 21, 2005.

Dolliver, Mark. "They'd Like the Genes to Remain Unmodified," *Adweek*, January 22, 2007.

Economist. "Greener than You Thought; GM Crops (Genetically Modified Sugar Beet Is Good for the Environment)," January 22, 2005.

Fernandez-Cornejo, Jorge. "U.S. Farmers Increase Adoption of Genetically Engineered Crops and Favor Multiple Traits," *Amber Waves*, September 2007.

Gunther, Marc. "Attack of the Mutant Rice," *Fortune*, July 9, 2007.

Los, Fraser. "The Terminator: The Next Extreme in GMO Could Undo 10,000 Years of Traditional Agriculture," *Alternatives Journal*, August 1, 2006.

Menard, Ryan. "Cloned Meat: Do We Know Enough About It? FDA Says It's OK, but Shoppers Aren't So Sure," *Patriot Ledger*, December 30, 2006.

Mesnage, Marion, and Martin Illsley. "Biotechnology: Out of the Labs and into Every Industry," *US Business Review*, March 2007.

Milano, Carol. "What's Happening to Your Food? How Genetic Engineering Is Changing What's on Your Plate," *Current Health 2*, April/May 2007.

Mukherjee, Andy. "Biotech Will Help China Reclaim Land, Grow Food," *Vancouver Sun*, September 10, 2007.

O'Neill, Graeme. "Gaining Ground: Debating the Growing Impact of GM Agriculture: Over a Decade Since the First Genetically Modified Crops Were Developed and Grown, Their Environmental and Production Credentials Are Being Better Assessed as Land Area Under GM Crops Expands. But the Role of GM Agriculture in the 21st Century Is Still Being Fiercely Debated," *Ecos*, February/March 2007.

Pollan, Michael. "No Bar Code: The Next Revolution in Food Is Just Around the Corner," *Mother Jones*, May/June 2006.

Popp, Trey. "God and the New Foodstuffs," *Science & Spirit*, March/April 2006.

Raney, Terri. "Economic Impact of Transgenic Crops in Developing Countries," *Current Opinion in Biotechnology*, April 2006.

Schwartz, Mark I. "Fear Versus Science Biotech Foods," *International Herald Tribune*, December 15, 2007.

Scrinis, Gyorgy. "Engineering the Foodchain," *Arena Magazine*, June/July 2005.

Smith, Jeffrey M. "Genetically Engineered Crops May Cause Human Disease," *Rachel's Democracy & Health News*, August 31, 2006.

Suk, J., A. Bruce, R. Gertz, C. Warkup, C.B.A. Whitelaw, A. Braun, C. Oram, E. Rodríguez-Cerezo, and I. Papatryfon, et al. "Dolly for Dinner? Assessing Commercial and Regulatory Trends in Cloned Livestock," *Nature Biotechnology*, January 2007.

Turner, Lisa. "Playing with Our Food," *Better Nutrition*, April 2007.

Van Eenennaam, Alison L. "Genetic Engineering and Animal Agriculture," University of California, Division of Agriculture and Natural Resources, publication no. 8184, Genetic Engineering Fact Sheet 7, 2005. http://anrcatalog/ucdavis.edu/pdf/8184.pdf.

Vartan, Starre. "Ah-tchoo! Do Genetically Modified Foods Cause Allergies?" *E*, November/December 2006.

Walters, Reece. "Crime, Bio-agriculture and the Exploitation of Hunger," *British Journal of Criminology*, January 2006.

Web Sites

Alliance for Better Foods (www.betterfoods.org). The Alliance for Better Foods is composed of a diverse group of farmers, scientists, grocers, processors, distributors, and food technologists who support biotechnology as a safe way to increase the world's food supply. Its Web site provides information about the development of plant biotechnology, the environmental benefits of genetically engineered crops, and the potential of genetically engineered foods to eliminate world hunger and malnutrition.

The Campaign to Label Genetically Engineered Foods (www.thecampaign.org). The campaign is a nonprofit political advocacy organization concerned with the inadequate testing of genetically engineered food crops. Using a national grassroots consumer campaign, it lobbies Congress to pass legislation requiring the labeling of genetically engineered foods. Activist and educational tools can be found on its Web site, including form letters to send letters to the U.S. Congress, government agencies, grocery stores, and food manufacturers.

Food and Agriculture Organization (www.fao.org/index_en.htm). Founded in 1945, the FAO is a specialized agency of the United Nations that leads international efforts to defeat hunger in both developed and developing countries. The FAO acts as a neutral forum for policy debates and negotiations between nations with the goal of promoting agricultural productivity, improving nutrition, and bettering the lives of rural populations. Its Web site provides several databases, including FAOSTAT, which lists a wide variety of food and agriculture statistics for over two hundred countries.

National Center for Food & Agricultural Policy (www.ncfap.org/index.php). The NCFAP created a biotechnology assessment program to study the potential benefits of herbicide-tolerant plants to improve pest management in American farming. It has prepared numerous reports and articles on the ongoing public debate over the use of biotechnology in food production, including "Plant Biotechnology: Current and Potential Impact for Improving Pest Management in US Agriculture, an Analysis of 40 Case Studies."

World Health Organization (www.who.int/foodsafety/biotech/en). Organized as a specialized agency of the United Nations, the WHO's main objective is to ensure that all peoples attain the highest possible level of health. It acts as a coordinating authority between various nations on a variety of international public health topics, including the role of biotechnology and genetically modified foods in worldwide food consumption. Its Web site provides general information, related links, and discussions about genetically engineered organisms as well as a link to its 2002 study *Modern Food Biotechnology, Human Health and Development: An Evidence-Based Study*, which examines the human health implications of genetically modified organisms and food products.

Index

Brazil
    GM crops in, 9, 100–102,
        104–105
    hunger in, 65
    soil loss in, 116
    soybean cultivation in,
        114–115, 116
Breast implants, 42
Bt (*Bacillis thuringiensis*) toxin,
    18–23, 32, 77–78
Burke, Derek, 119
Bush, George W., 130
Busquin, Philippe, 56
Butanol, 123–124, 128
Butterflies, 118

C
Canada, 9, 12, 38–39
Cancer, 25, 28–29
Canola seeds, 75
Carabid beetles, 118
Carbon dioxide, 120–121
Cargill, 128
Charles, Daniel, 67
Chemicals, 65
China, 9, 103, 131
CIMMYT, 68, 72, 73
Climate change. *See* Global
    warming
Cloned products, 33–34, 70–73
Consumer protection, 44
Consumer rights, 35–36, 47–48
Conventional crops
    danger from, 15
    toxins in, 16
Cook, Ken, 130

Co-ordination Framework for
    Regulation of Biotechnology,
    13
Corn
    apomictic, 70–73
    cloning of, 70–73
    GM, 12, 14, 22–23
    reproduction, 69
Corporations, 79
Cotton, 12, 14, 22, 65
Cracker brands, 43
Crop disasters, 76
Crop rotation, 79
Cry1Ab, 21

D
da Silva, Luiz Inácio Lula,
    100–101, 104
Dangers, of GM foods, 17–23,
    94, 96
Delta & Pine Land Co., 97–98
Developing countries
    GM crops harm, 86–92
    GM crops help, 80–85
    hunger and malnutrition in,
        57, 87–88
Disease
    GM foods cause, 24–30
    new, 28
DNA, 7, 72, 108
    See also Genes
Dow corning, 42
DuPont, 128

E
Earth, ecology of, 77–78

prevalence of GM foods in, 32–33
Uruguay, 114

V

Vanhemelrijck, Johan, 130
Vavilov, Nikolai, 76
Vegetarian diet, 28–29
Vietnam, 103
Vitamin A, 81–82, 88
Vitamin B12, 28
Vitamins, 26, 27, 81–82

W

Wheat, 68–69

Whellamd, Melissa, 37
Whitworth, Katherine, 93
World Food Program, 79, 89
World Food Summit, 65
World Health Organization (WHO), 20, 42
World Trade Organization (WTO), 12, 60

Y

Yield Guard, 16, 21

Z

Zambia, 8, 56, 57, 89
Zimbabwe, 89

Picture Credits

Maury Aaseng, 14, 19, 29, 33, 43, 57, 69, 83, 95, 103, 111, 121

AFP/Getty Images, 117

AP Images, 13, 34, 54, 59, 84, 90, 96, 101, 129

Scott Barbour/Getty Images, 26

© Nigel Cattlin/Alamy, 109

Le Deodic David/Maxppp/Landov, 64

© Goss Images/Alamy, 70

© Nick Gregory/Alamy, 106

Chris Kleponis/Bloomberg News/Landov, 51

© Medical-on-line/Alamy, 77

© Vanessa Miles/Alamy, 40

© 67photo/Alamy, 123

© Inga Spence/Alamy, 21

© Mark Sykes/Alamy, 10

About the Editor

Jennifer L. Skancke lives and works in San Francisco. Aside from writing, she loves reading, HBO programming, learning Italian, hiking, camping, traveling, and laughing with friends.